I0696030

EL LIBRO PUBLISHER
LIBRO LIBRO
CHILDREN'S COLORING BOOKS

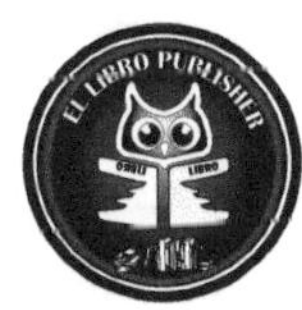

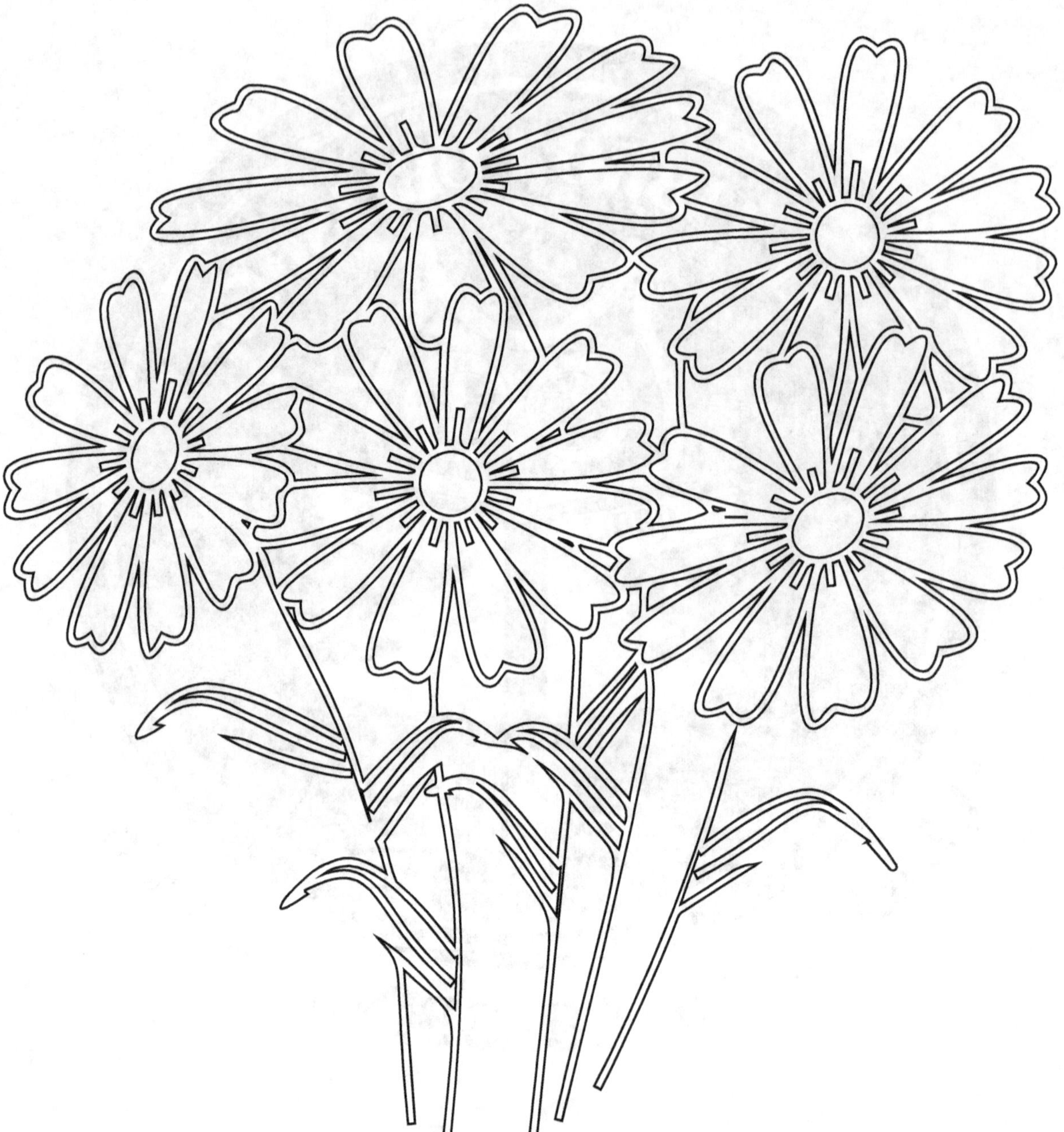

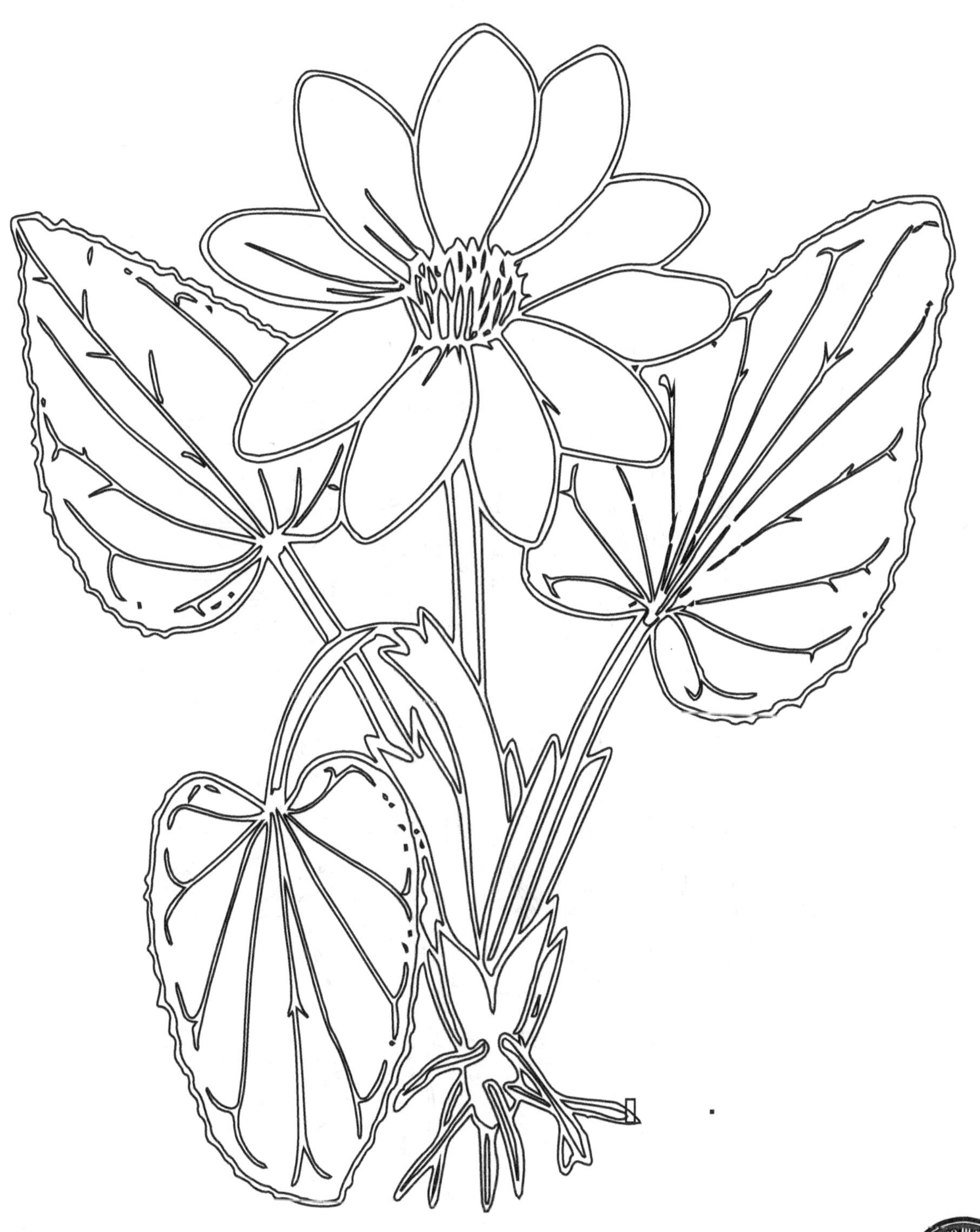

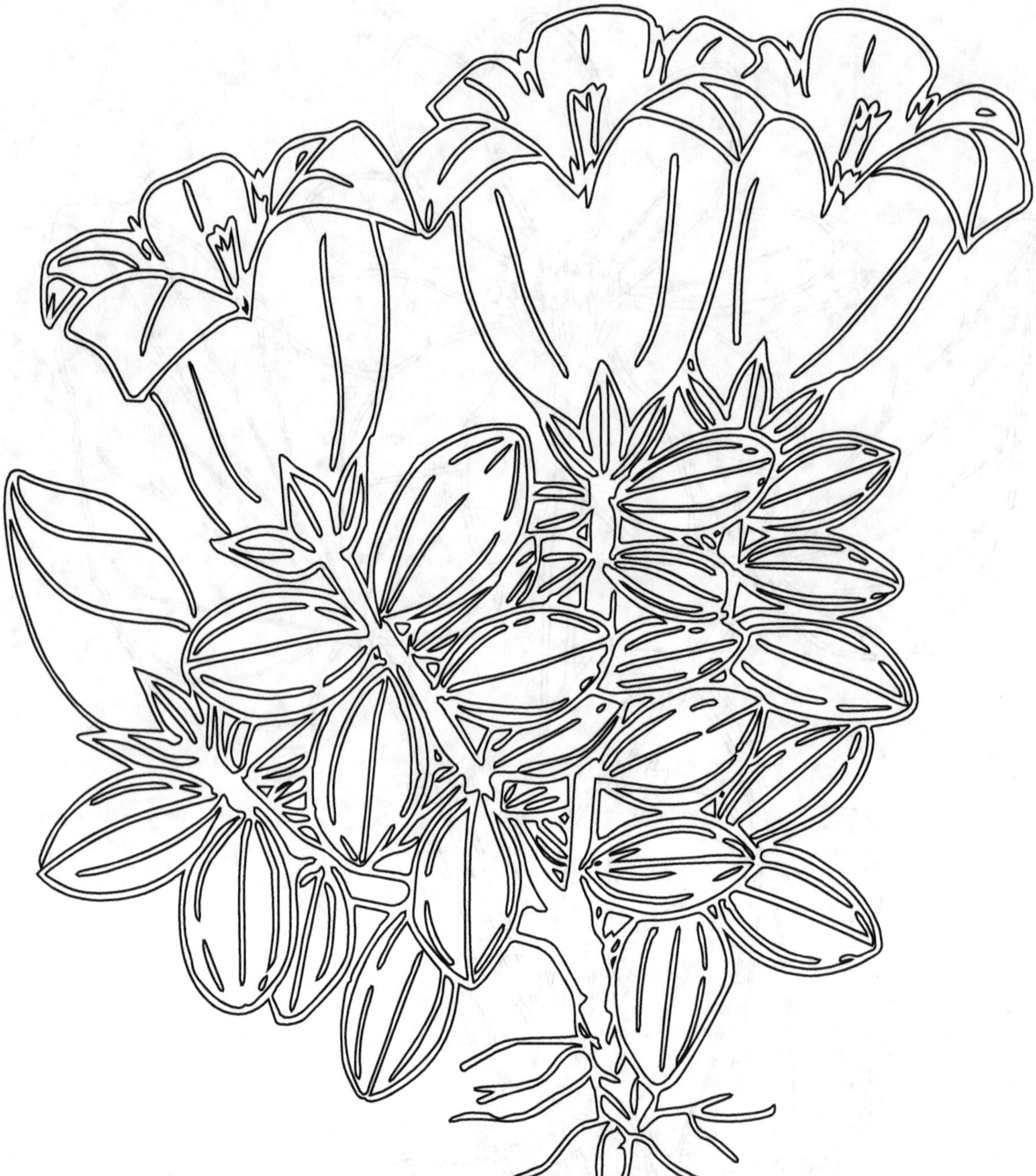

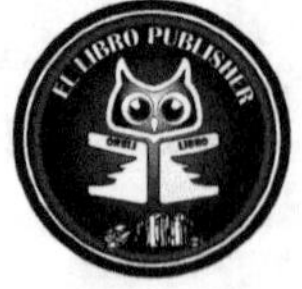

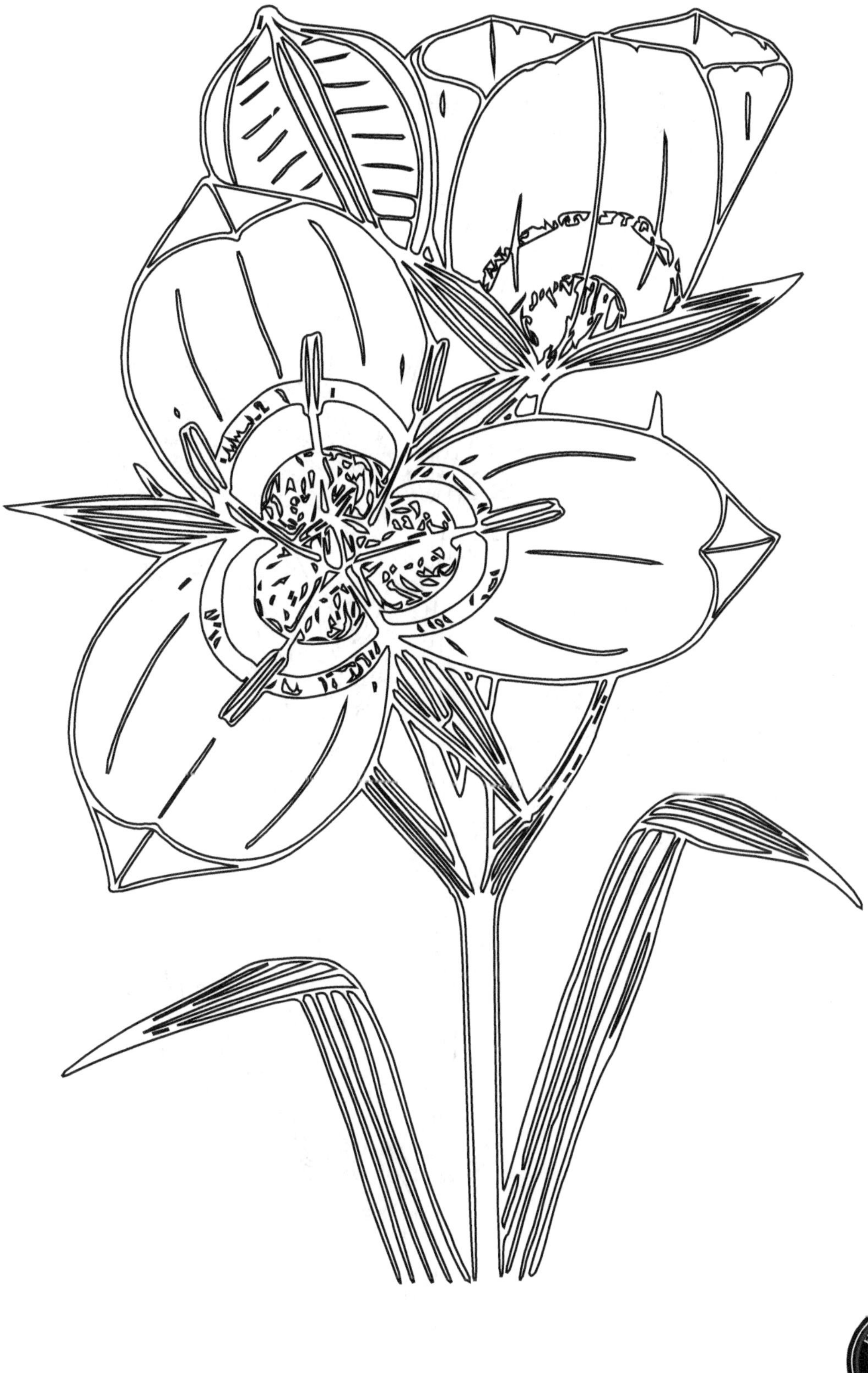

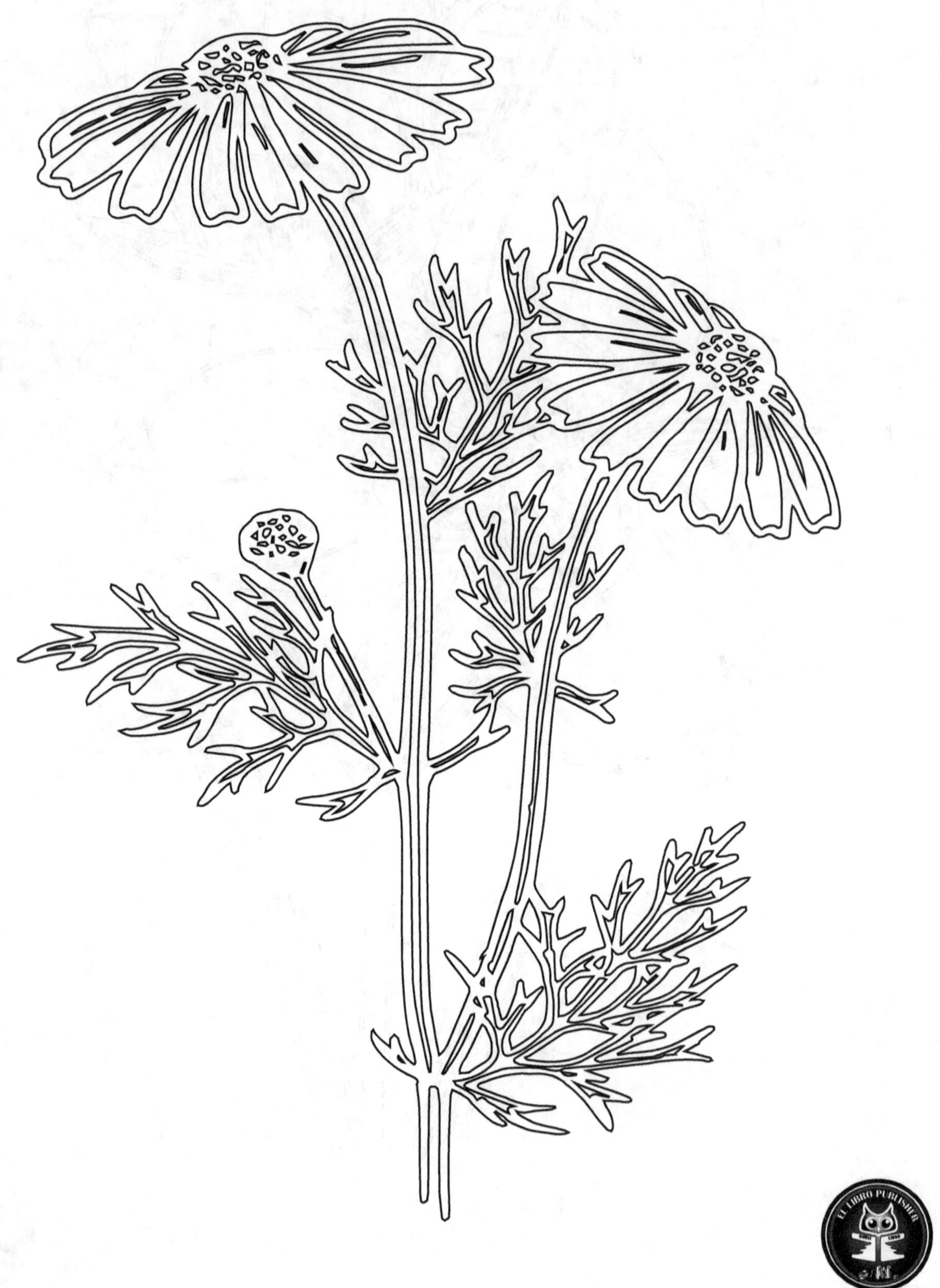

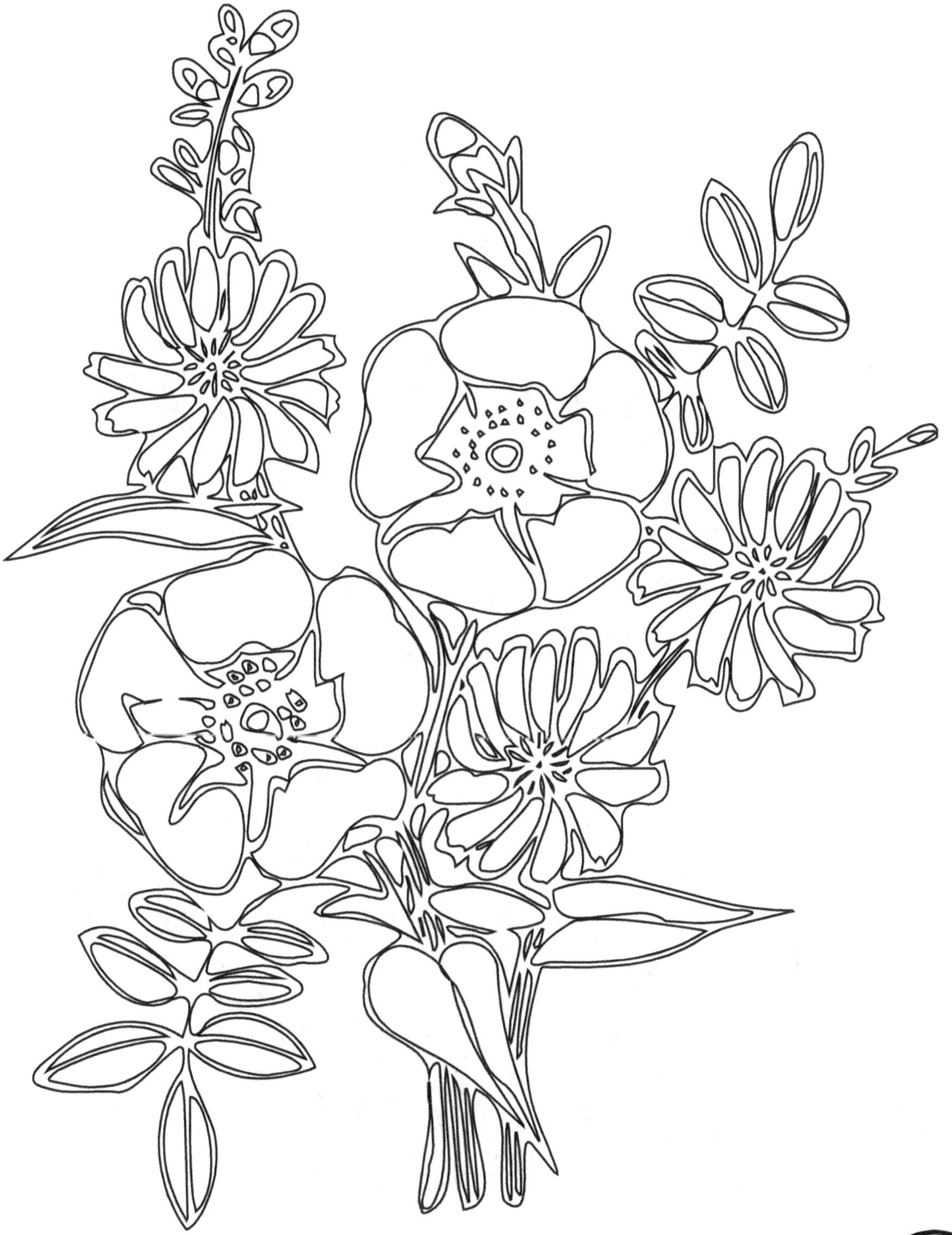

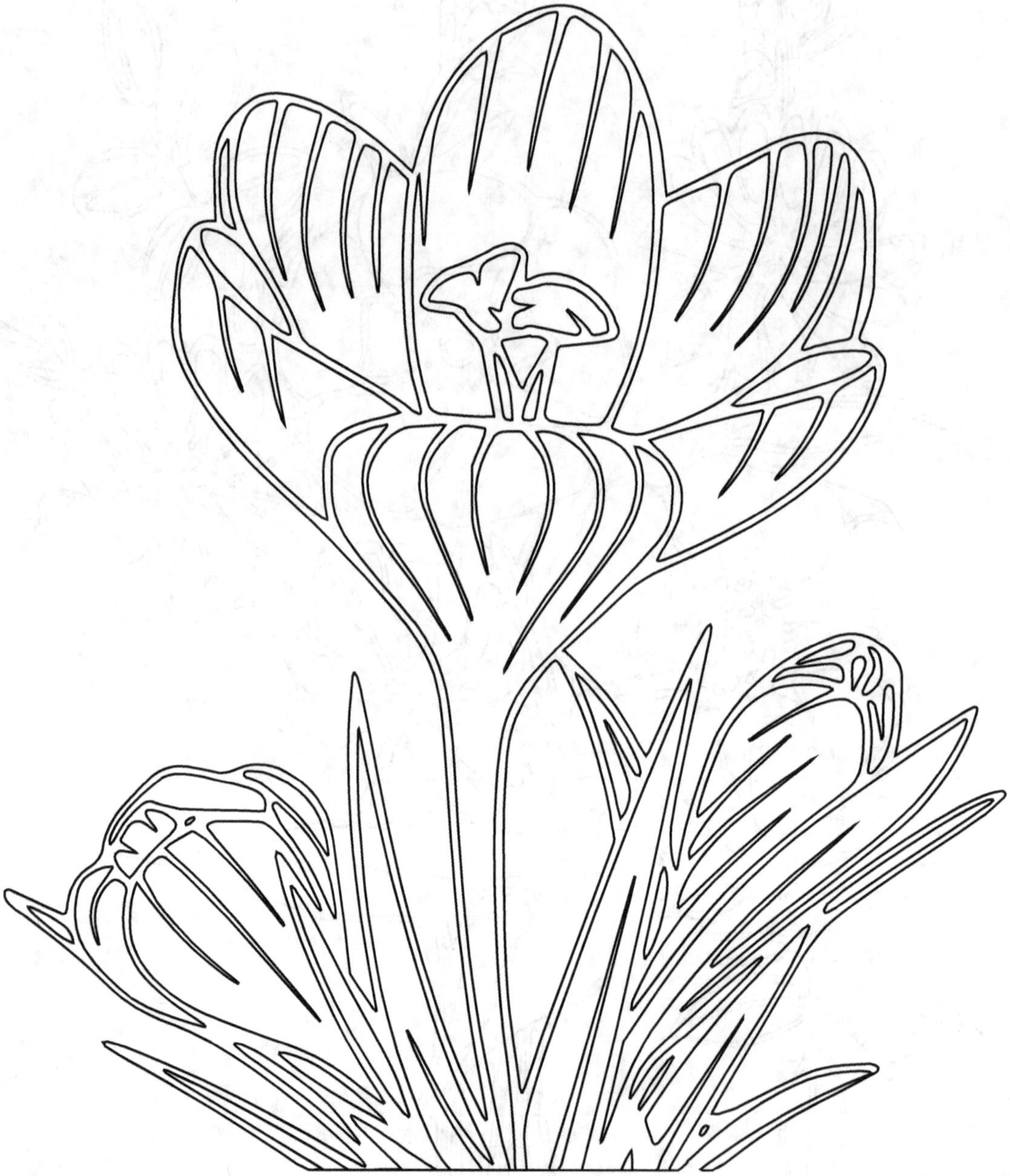

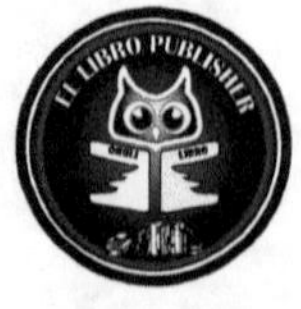

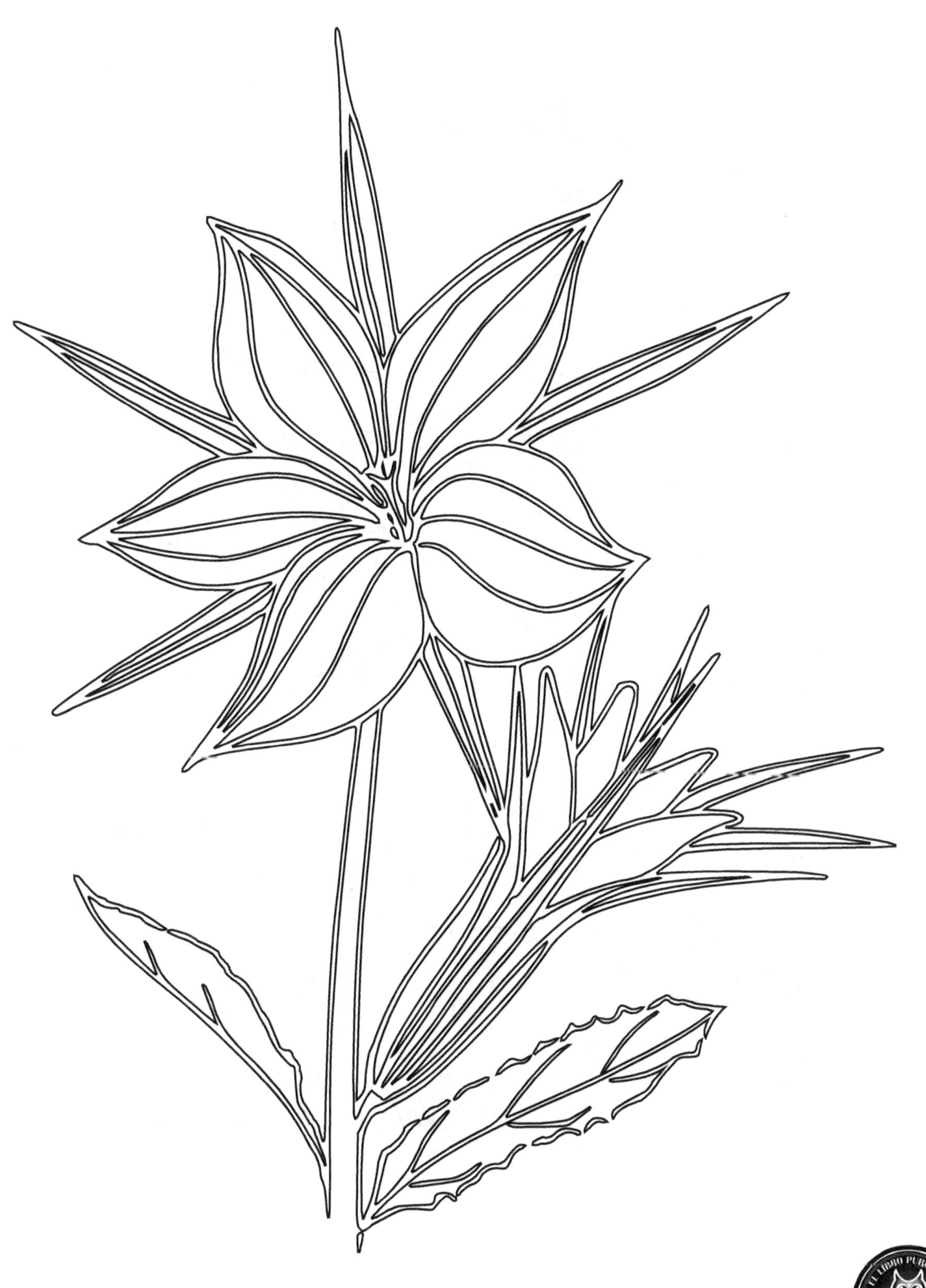

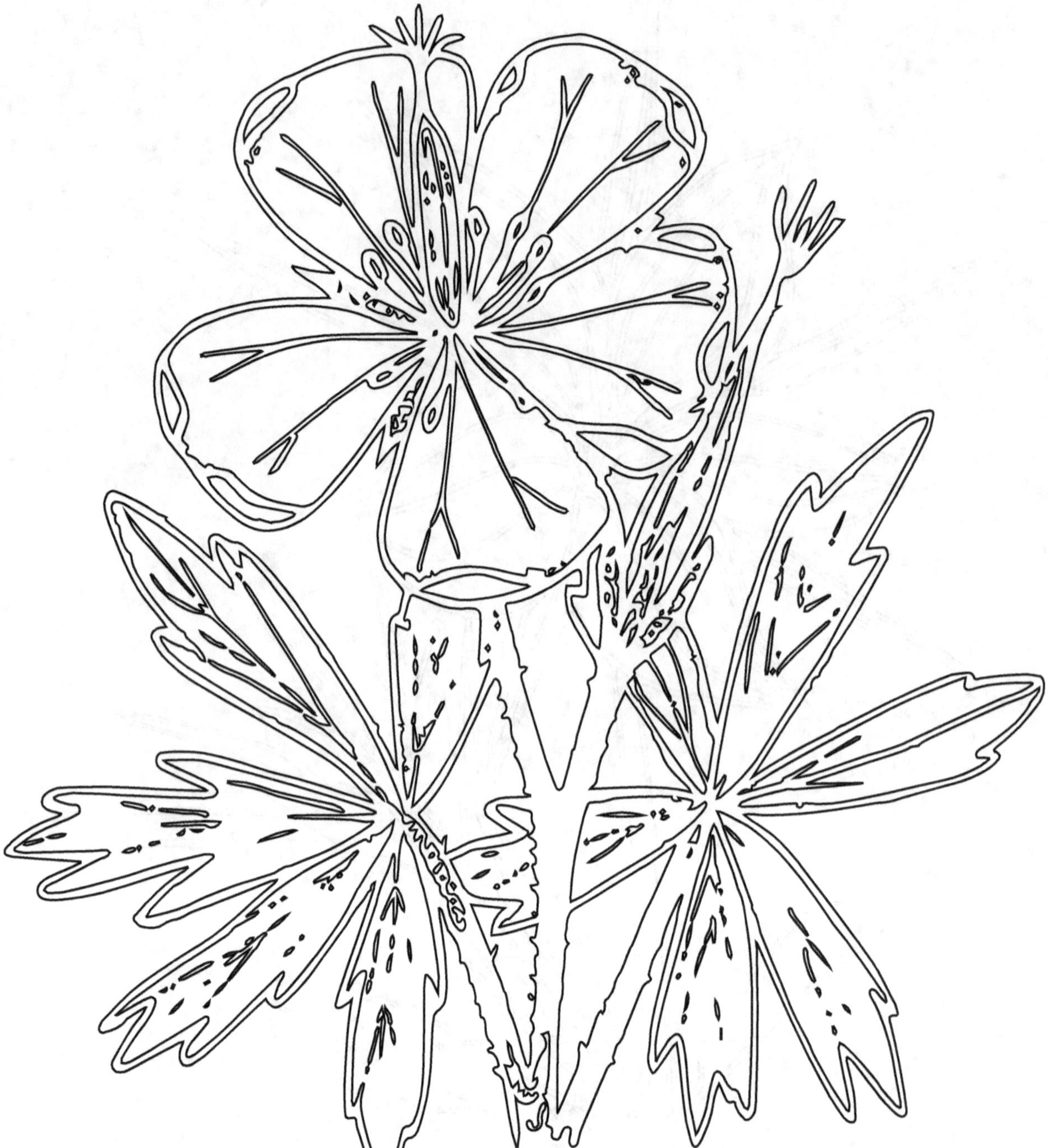

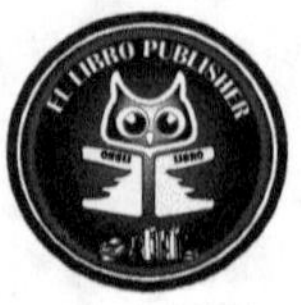

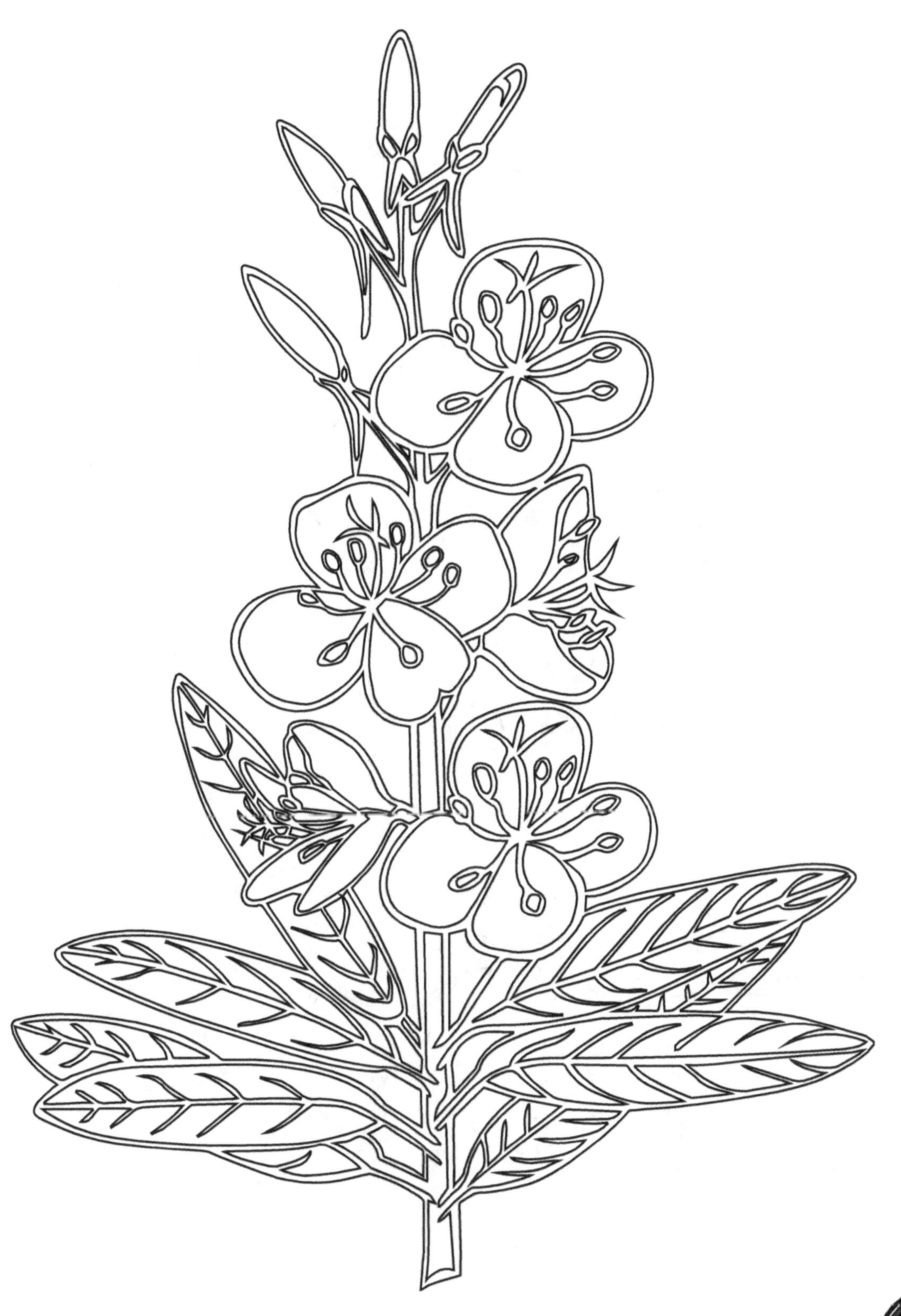

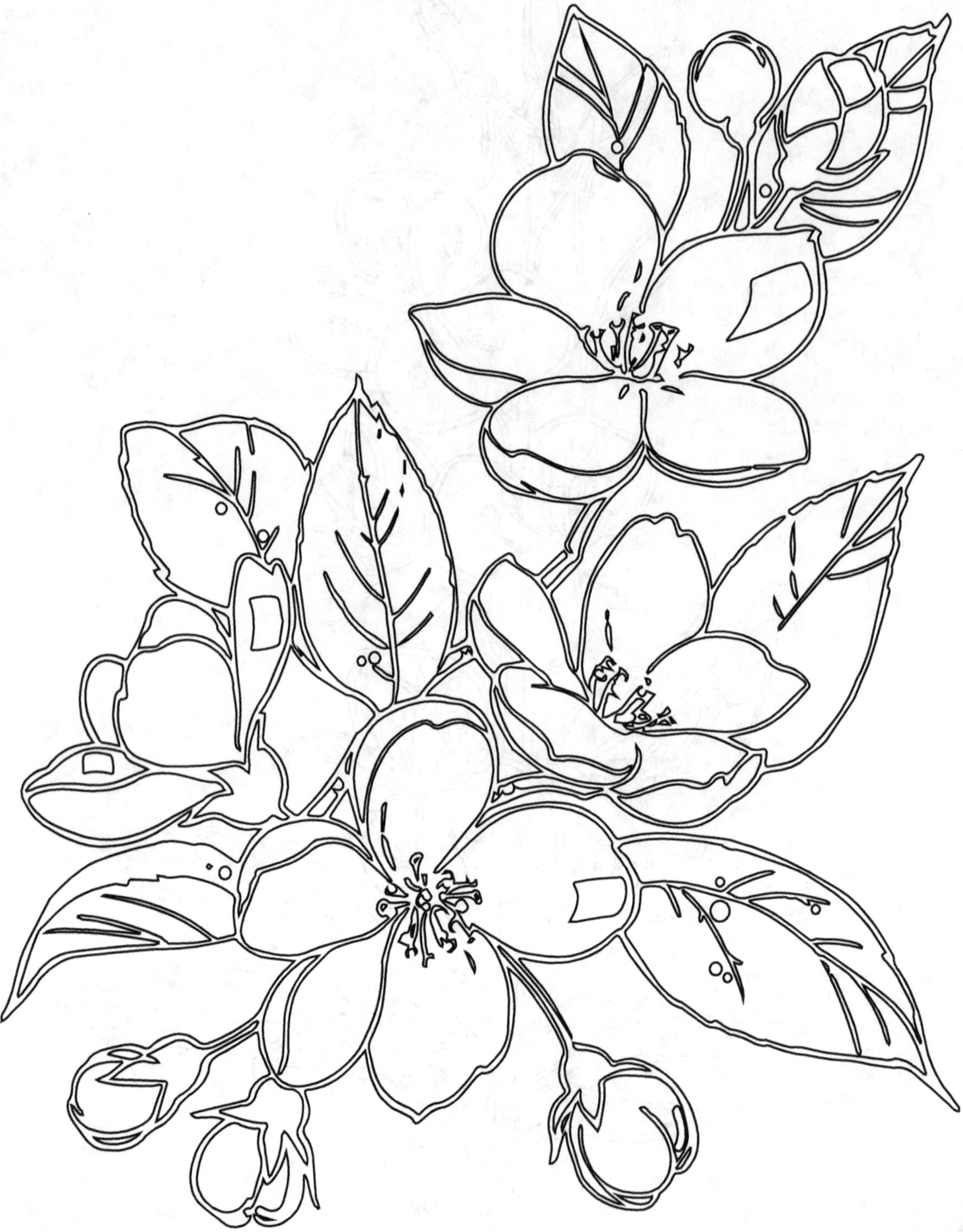

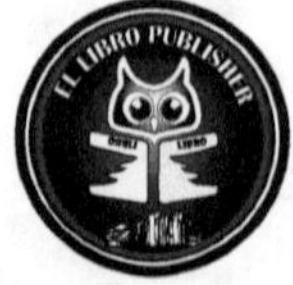

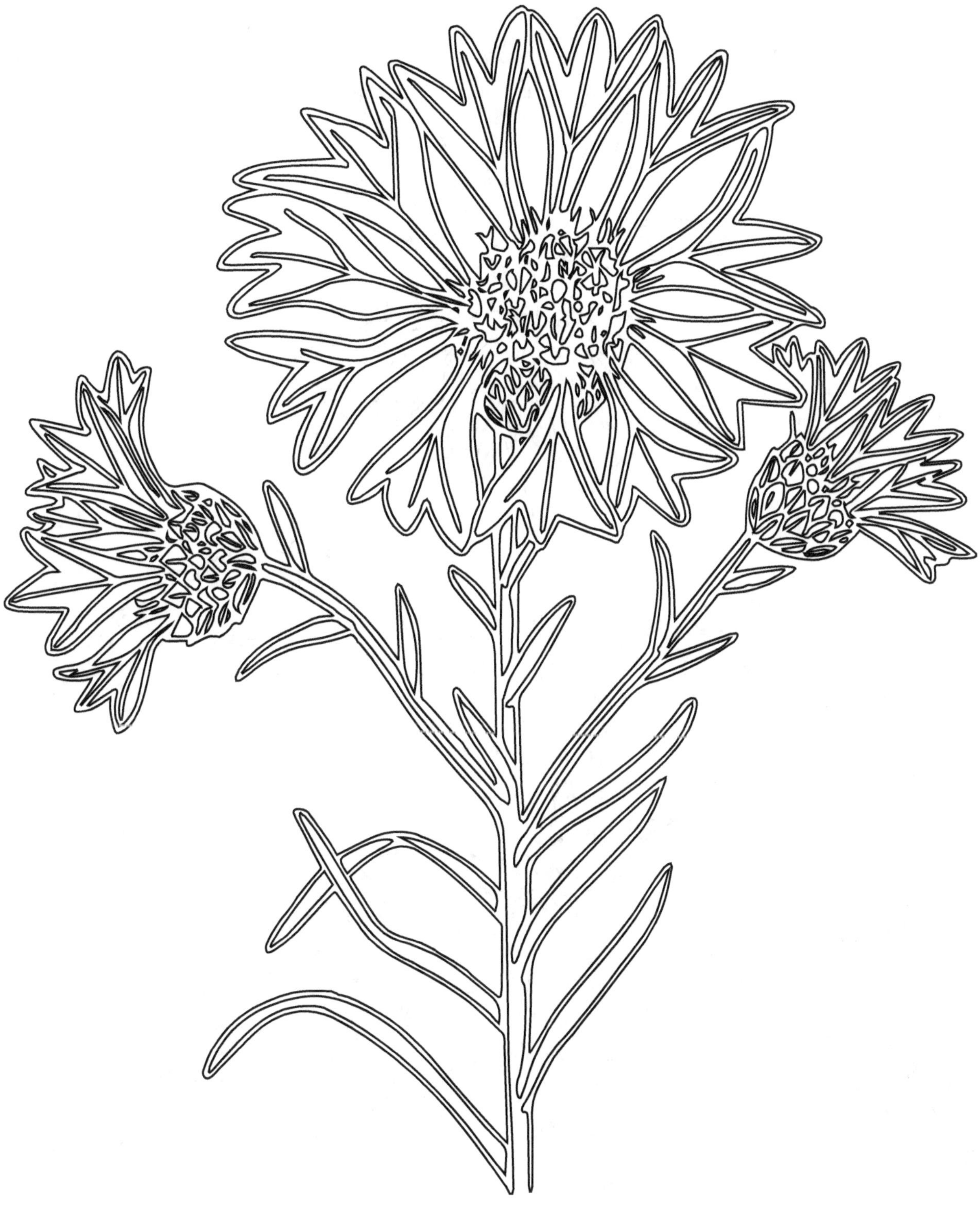

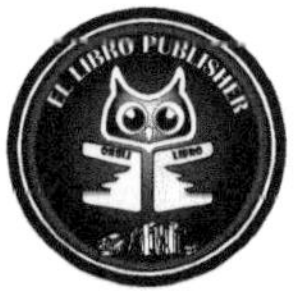

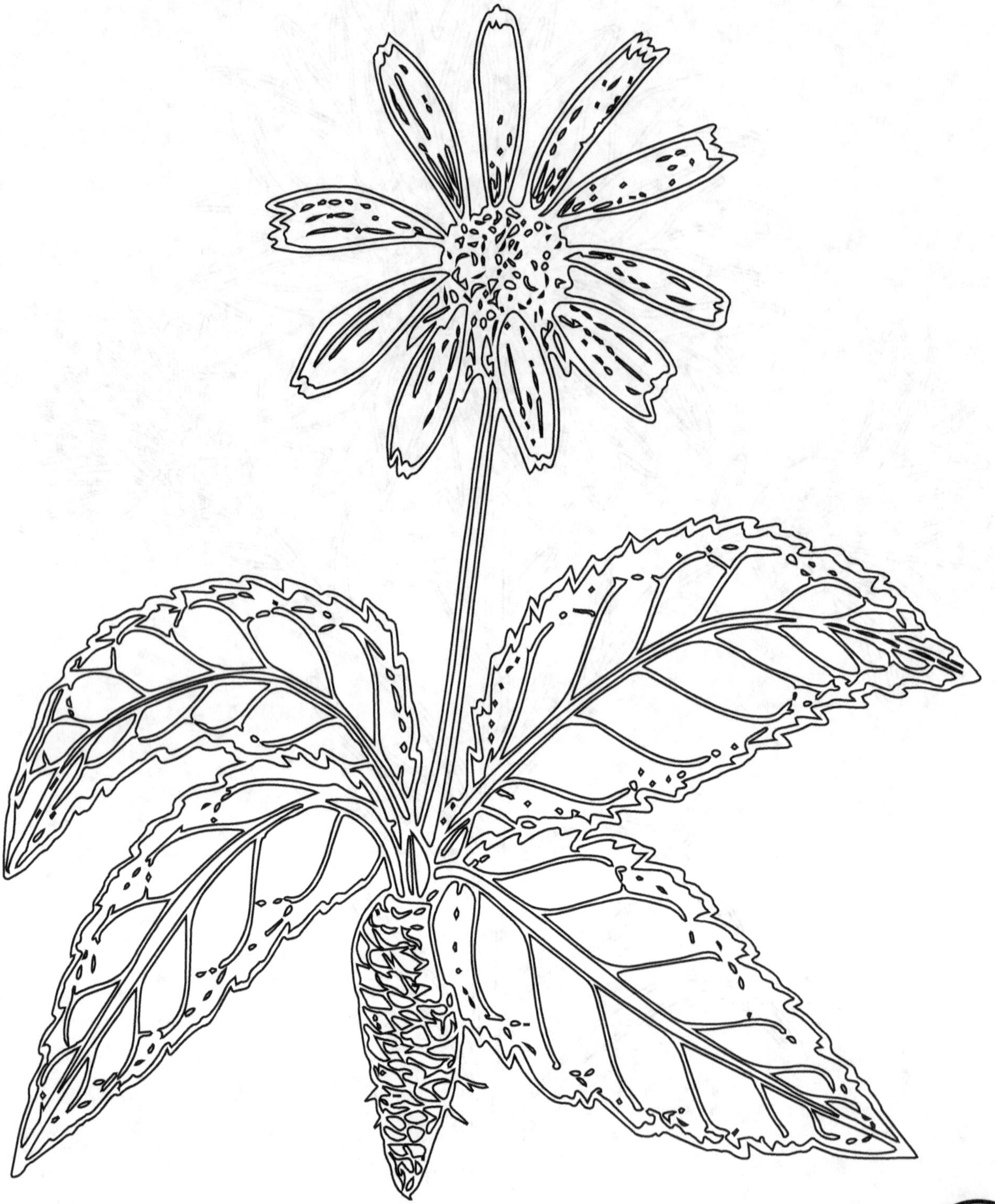

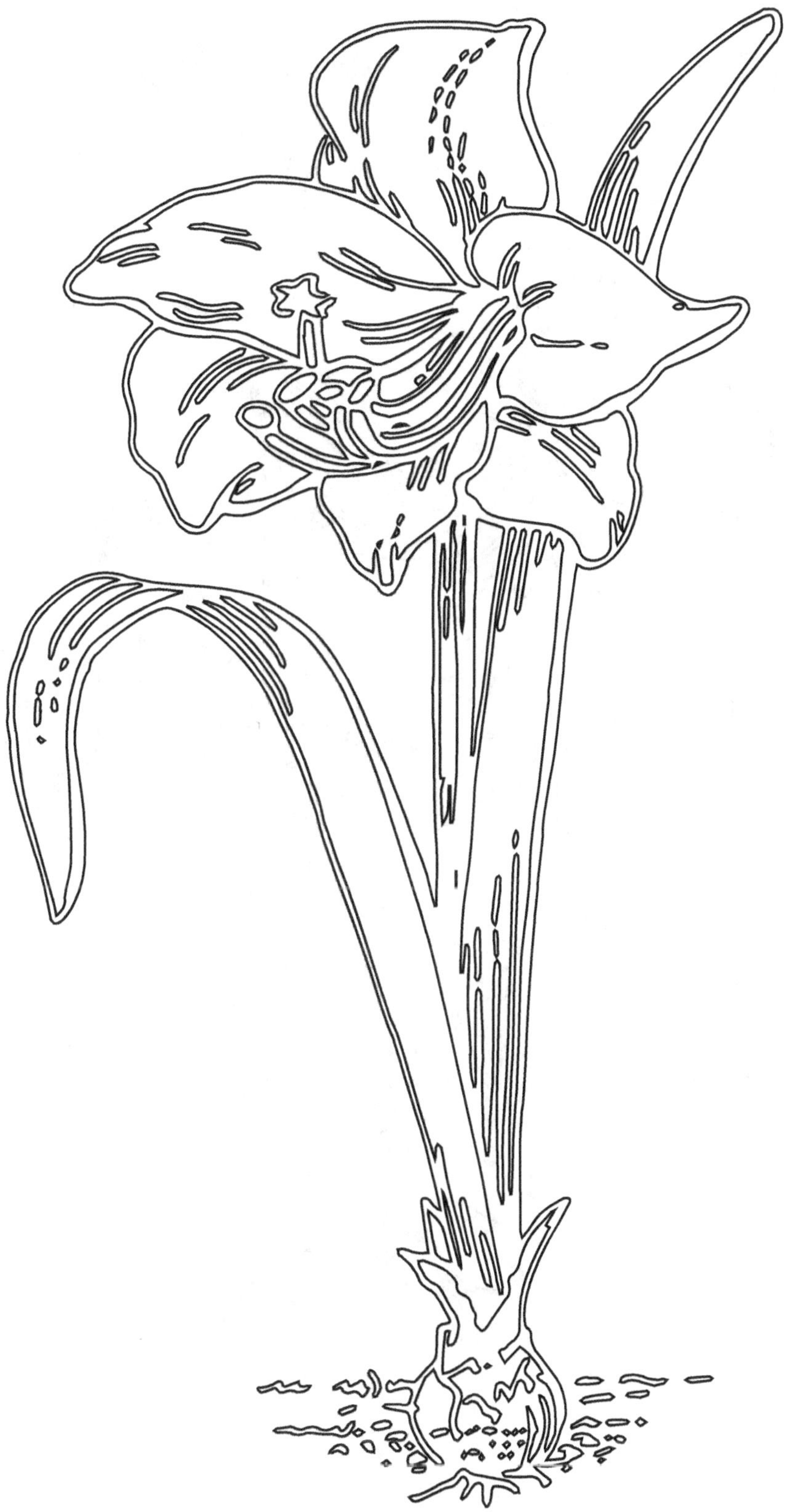

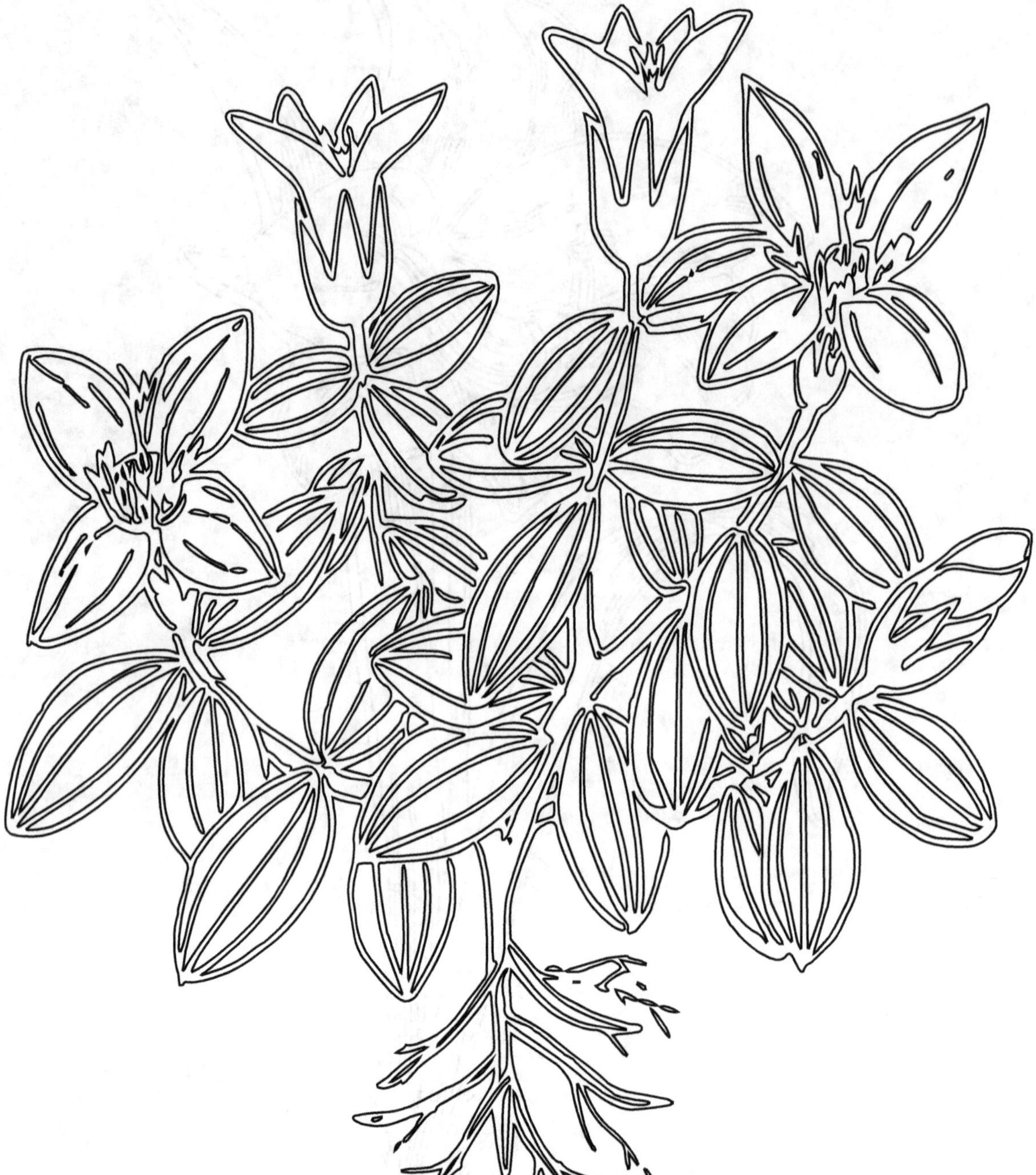

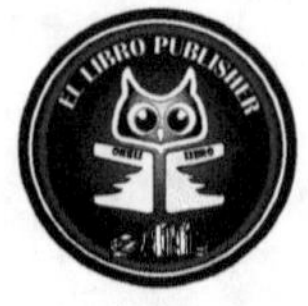

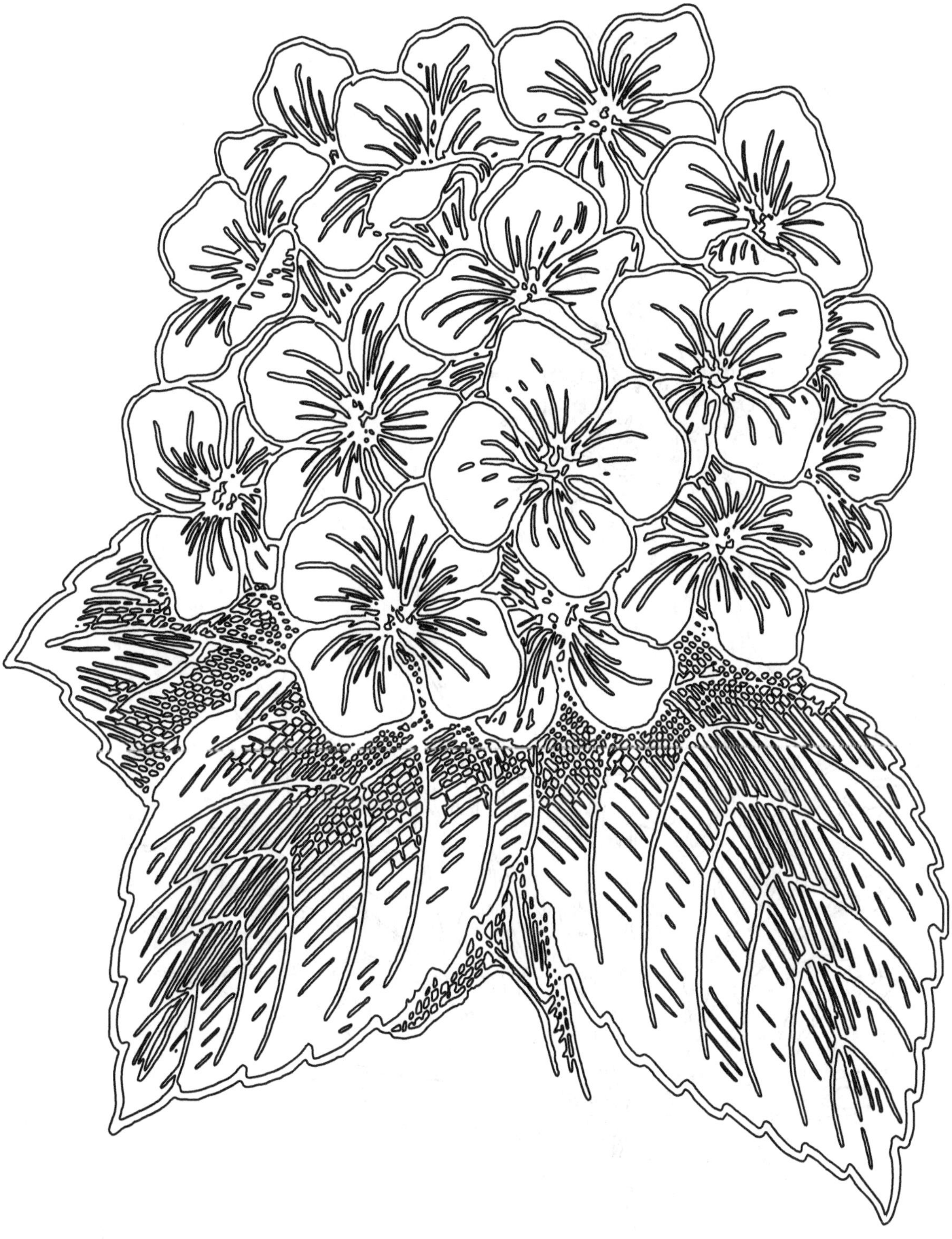

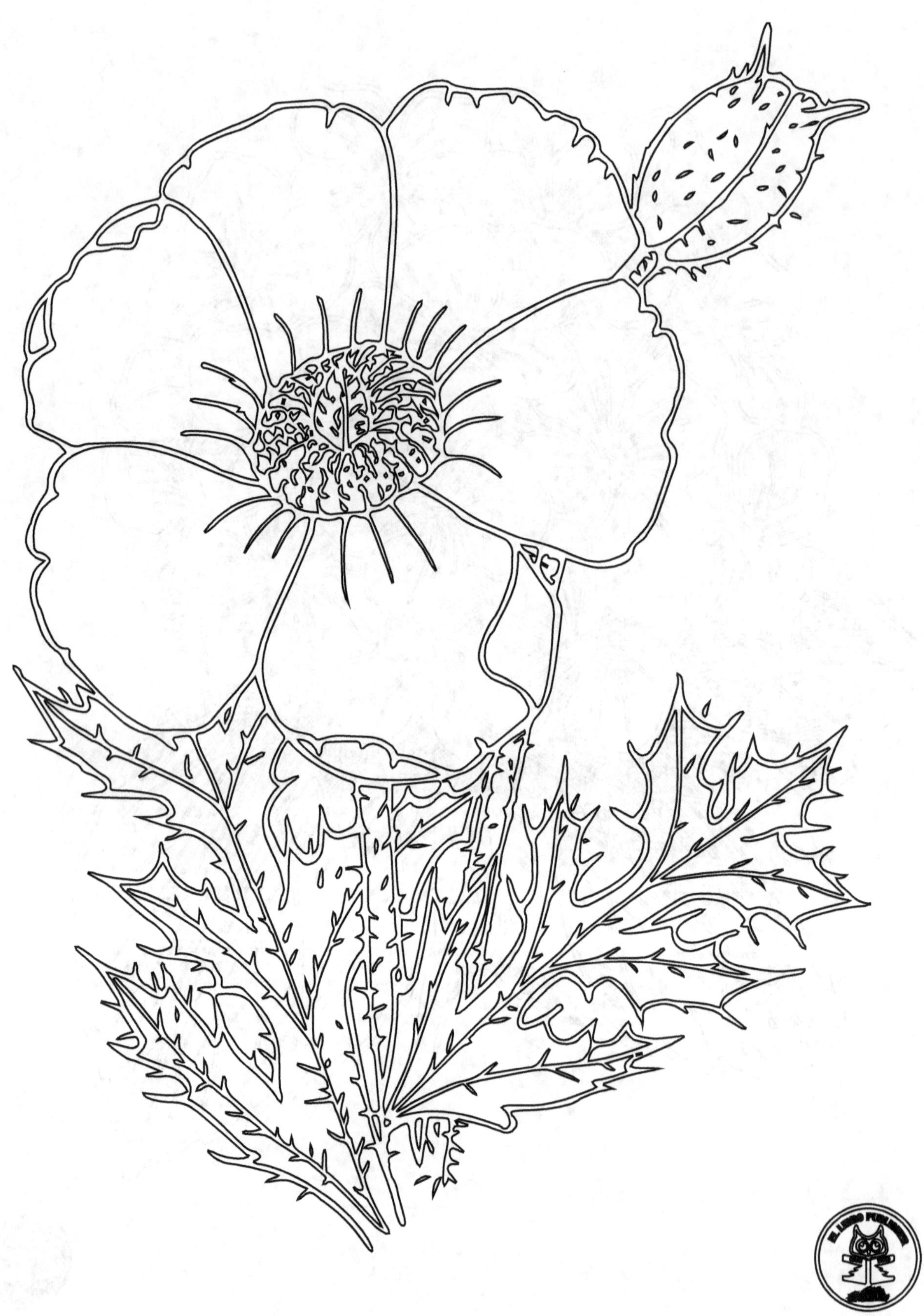

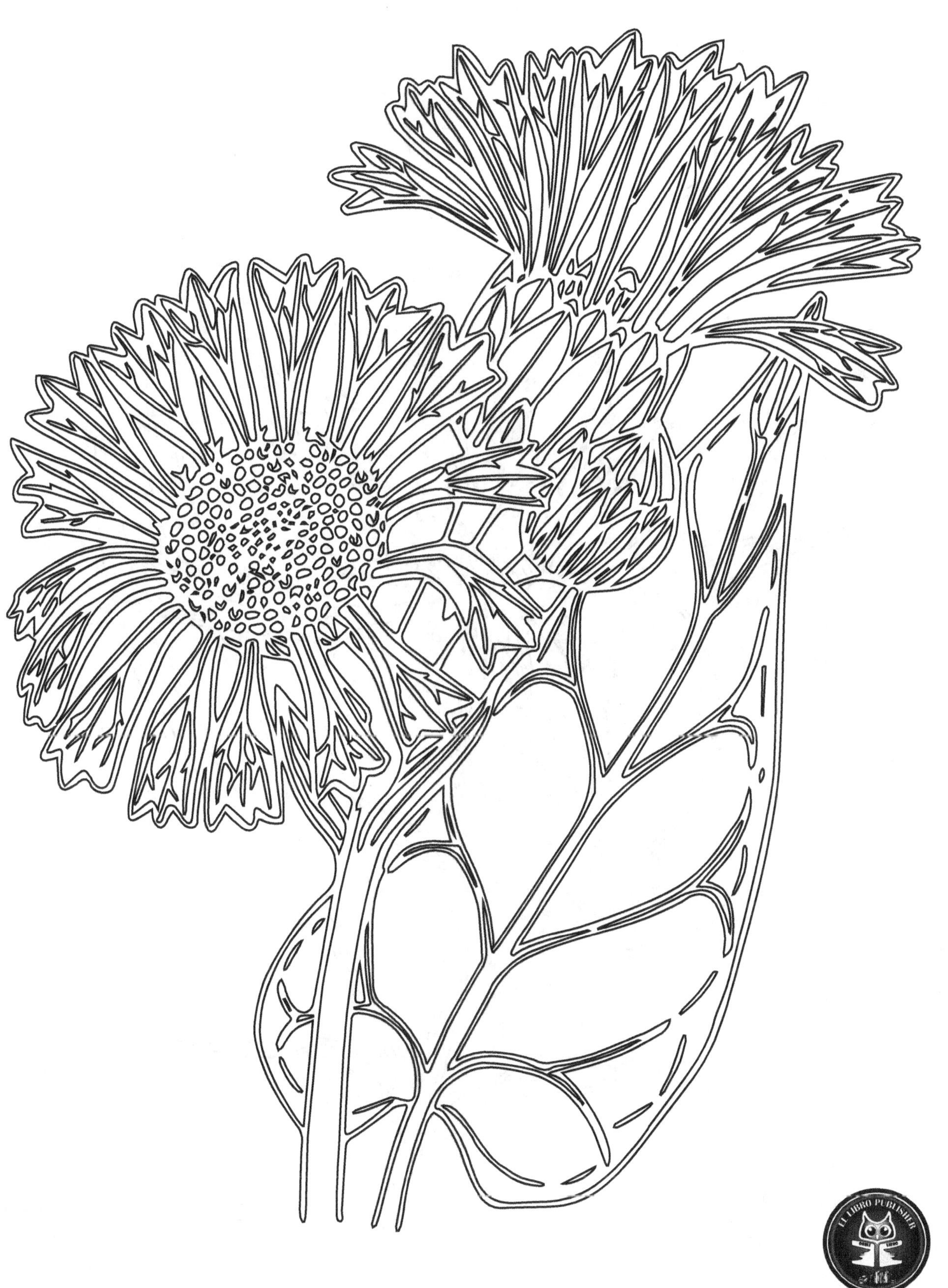

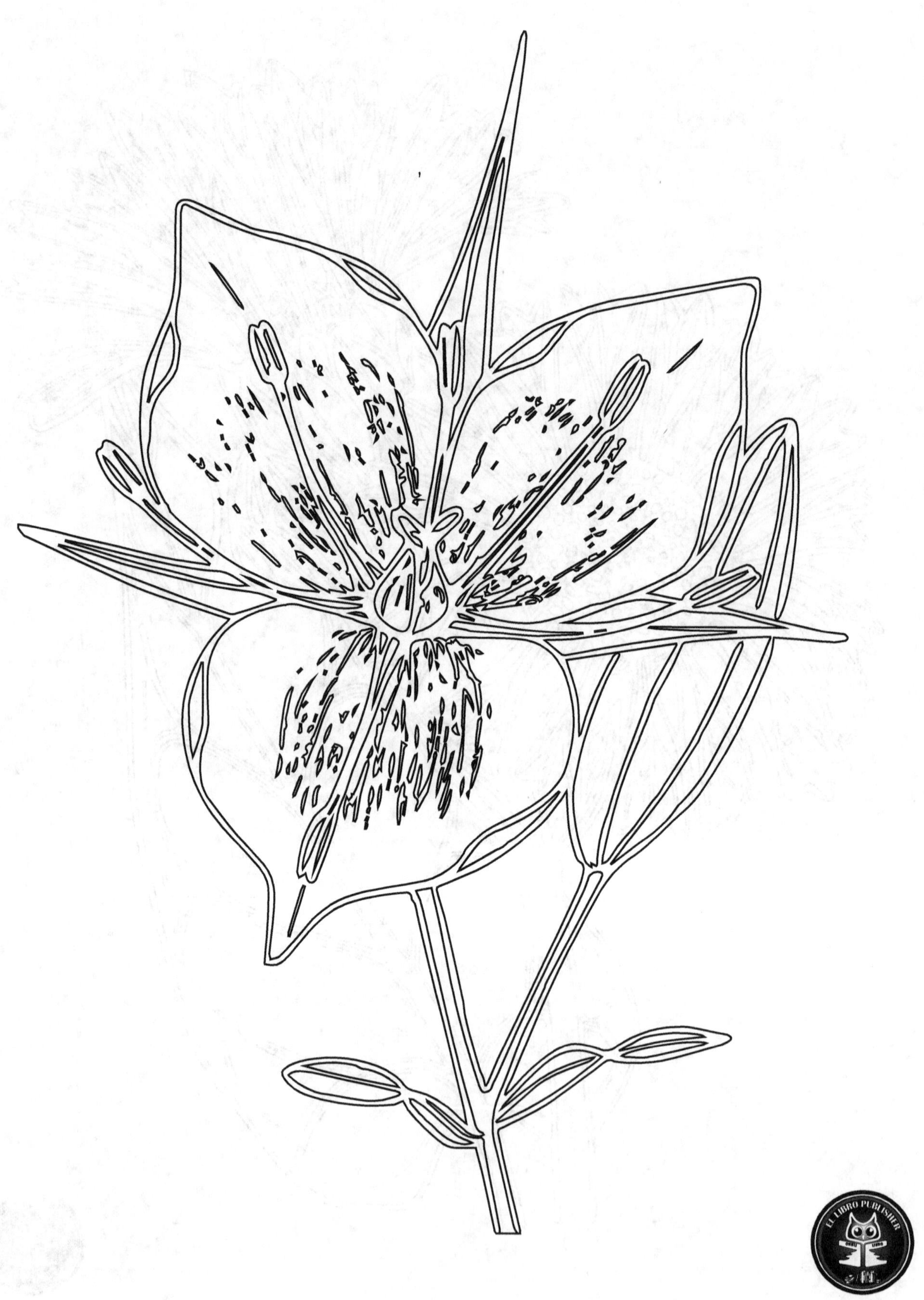

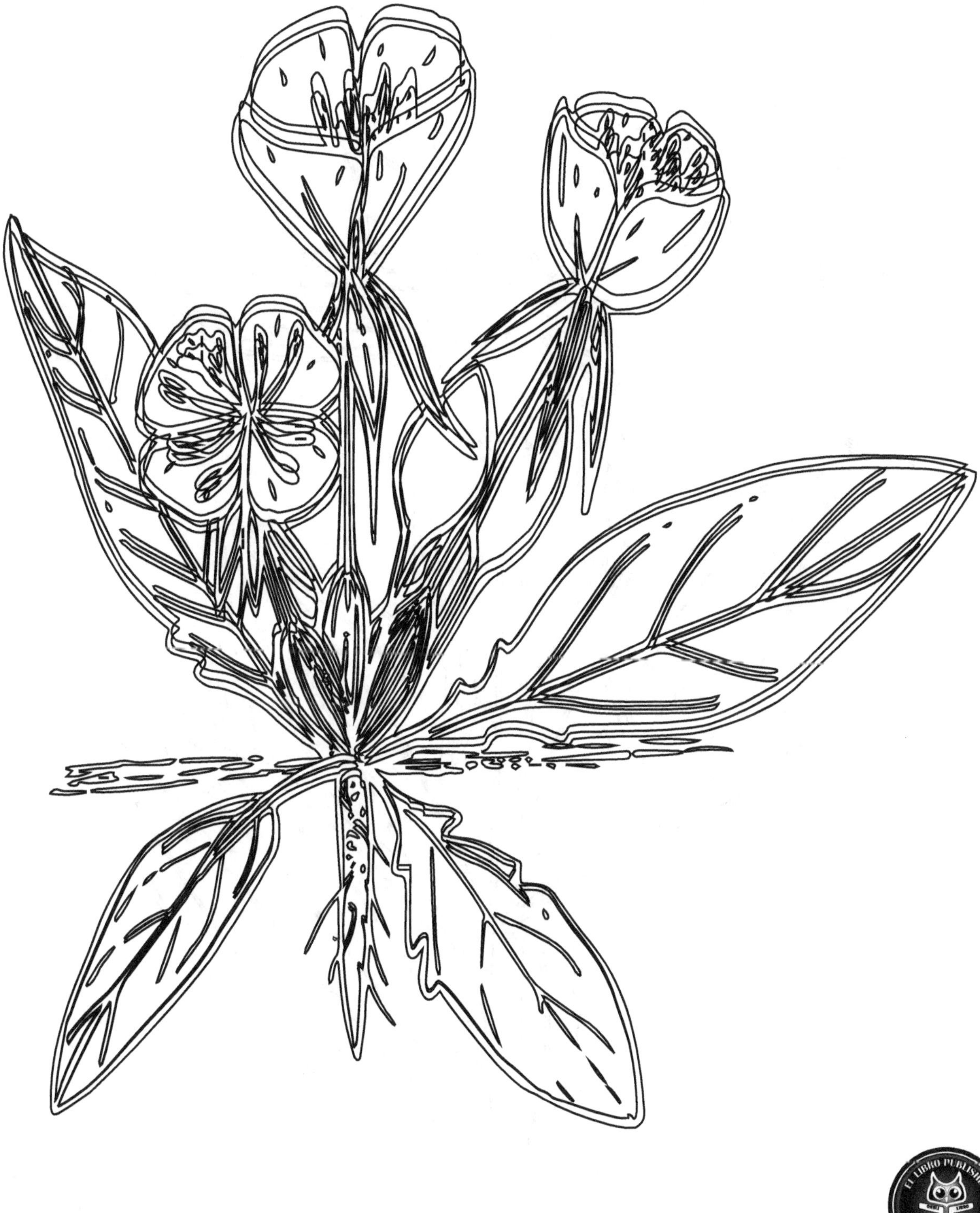

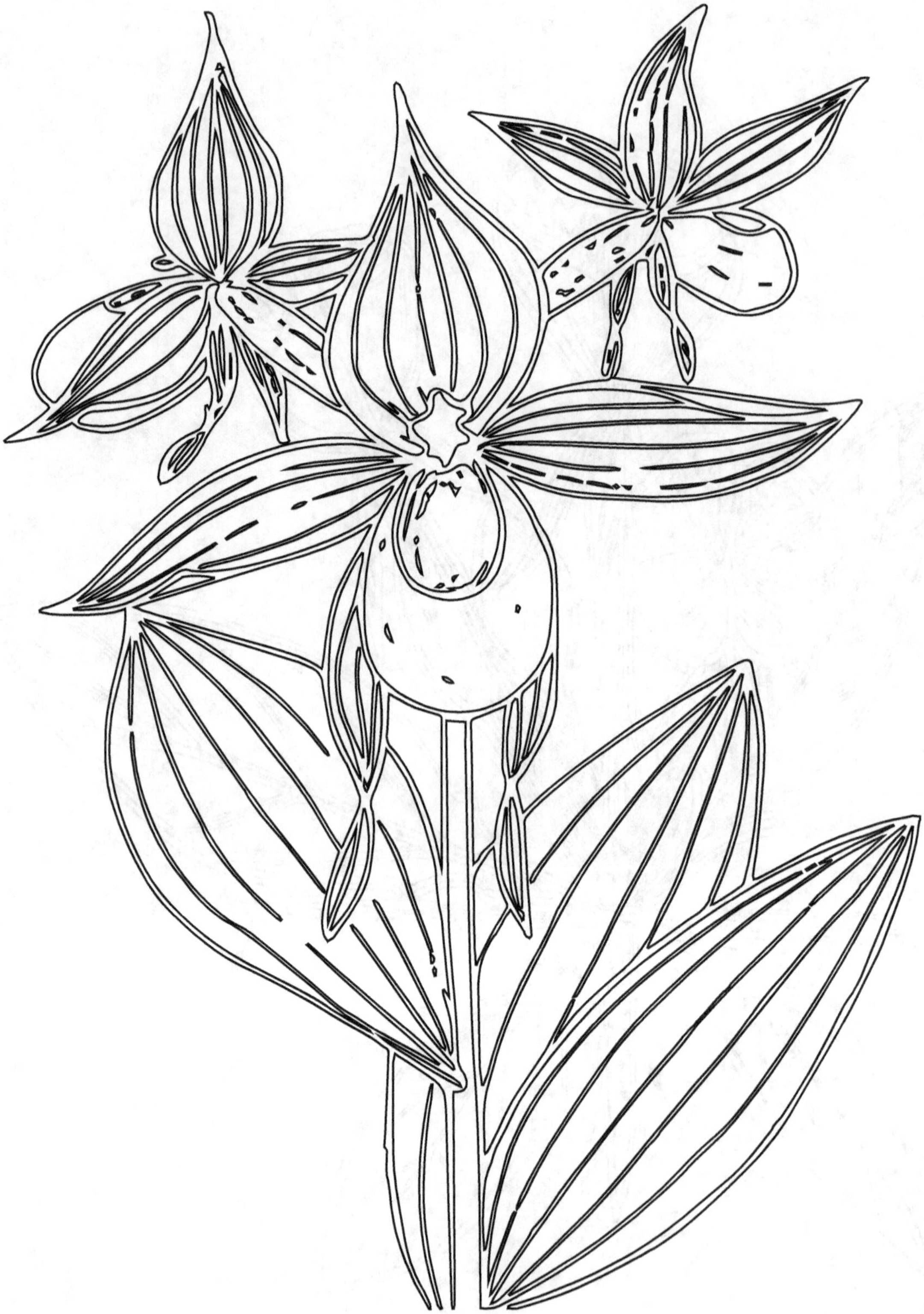

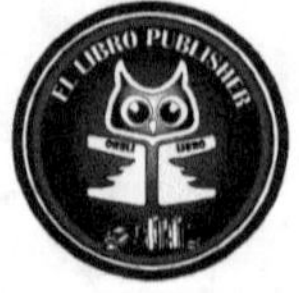

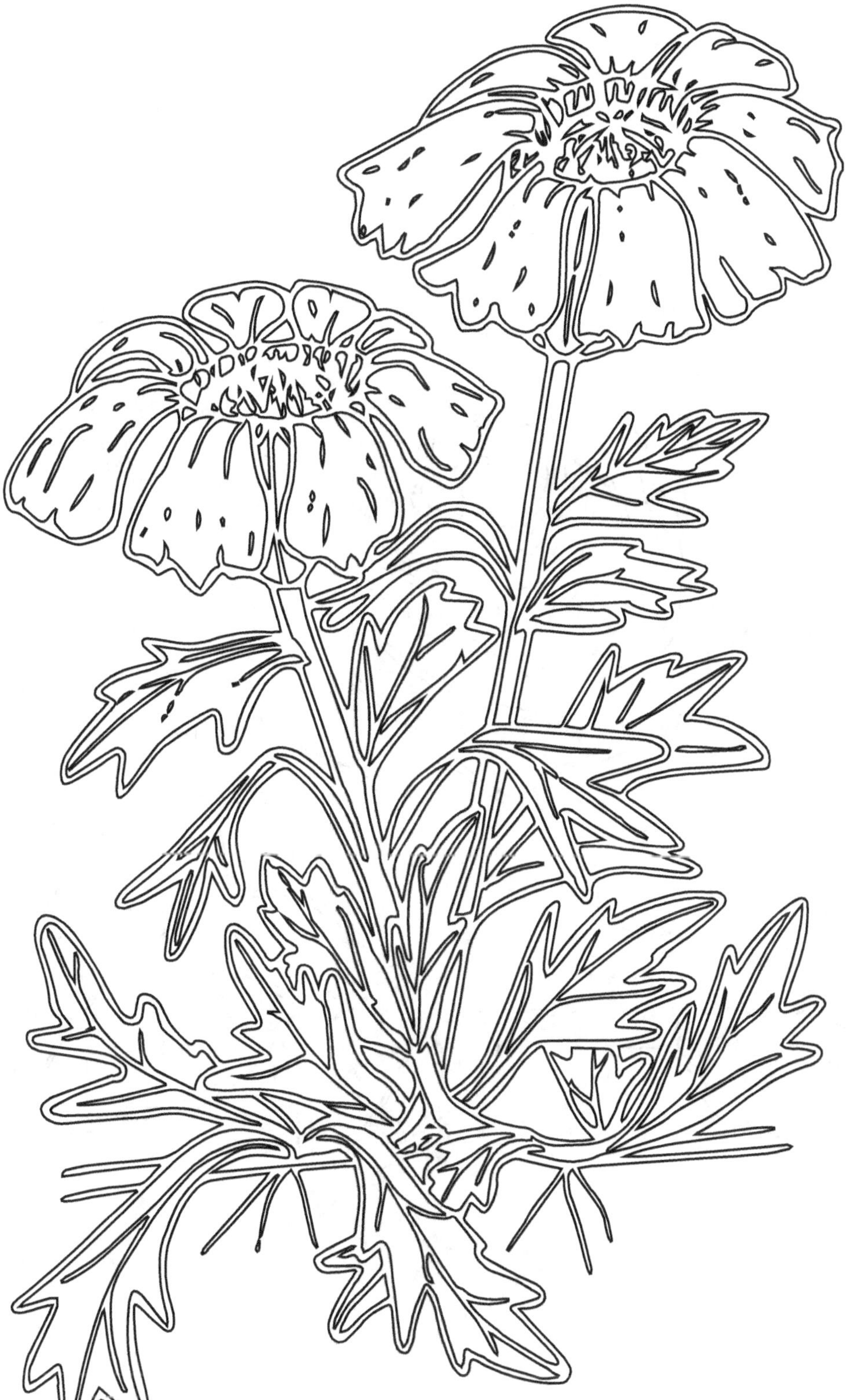

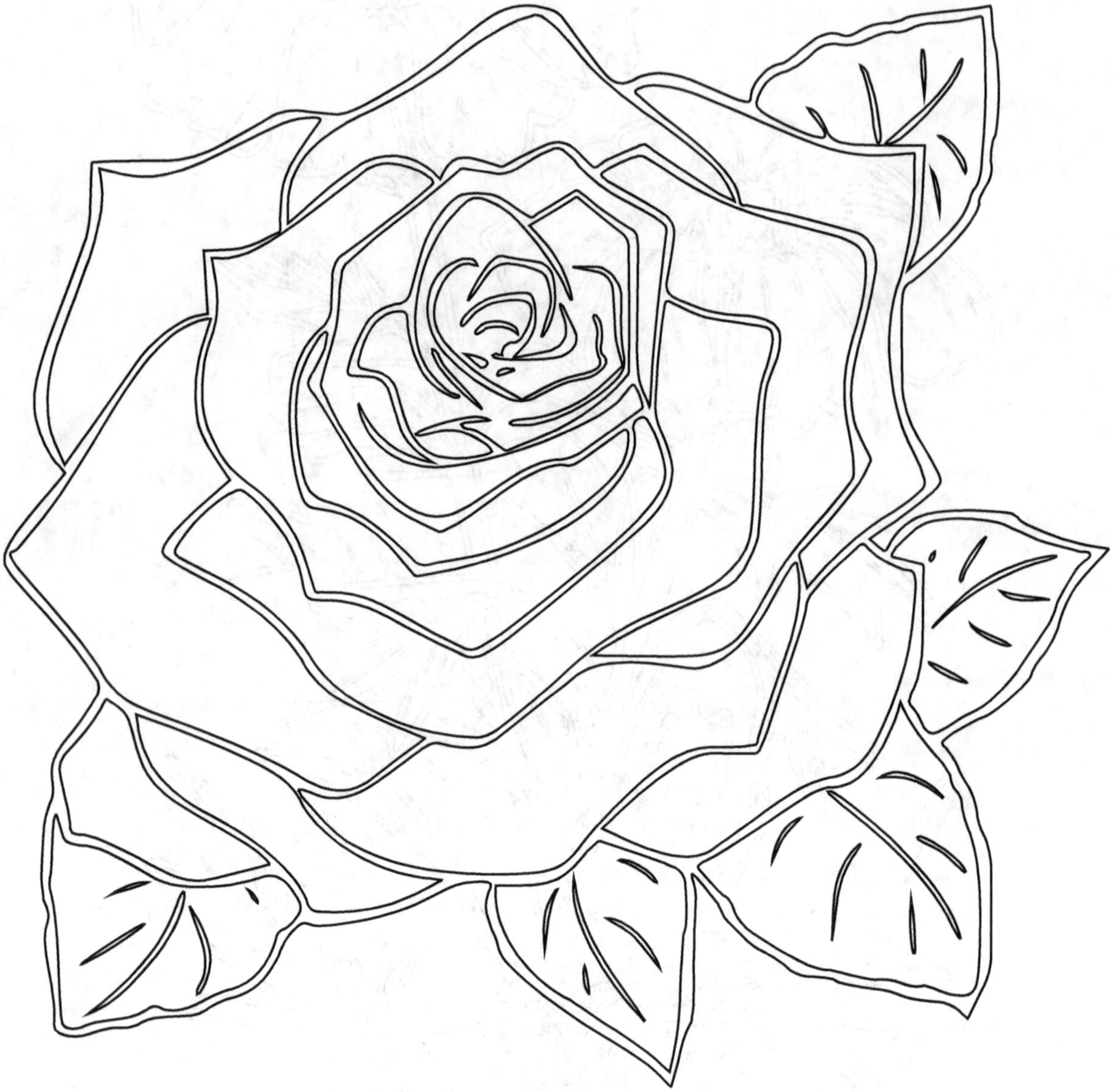

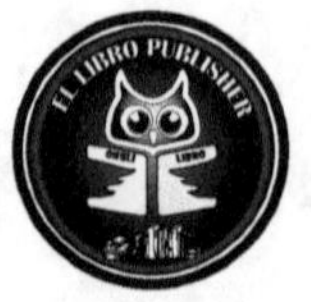

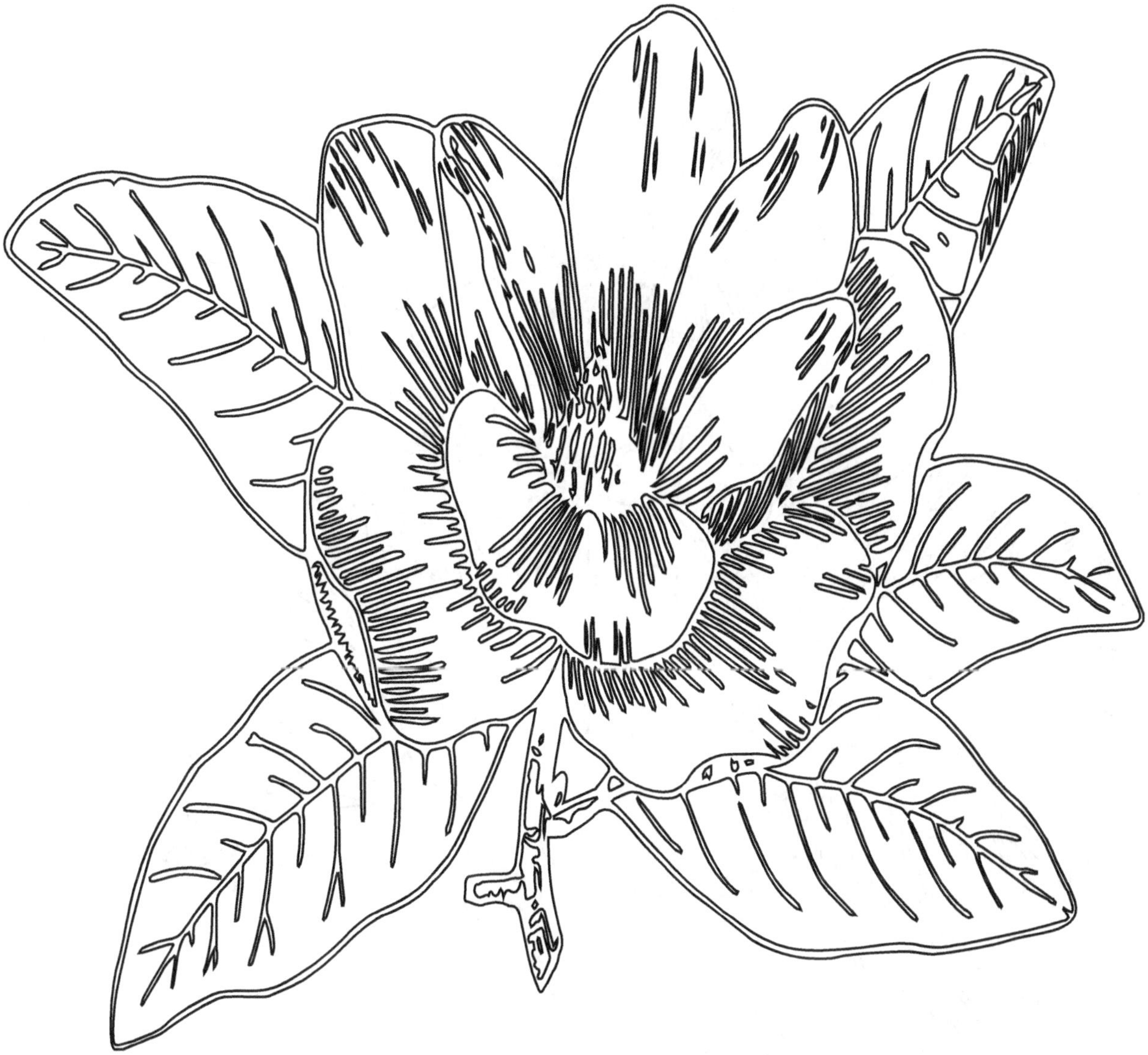

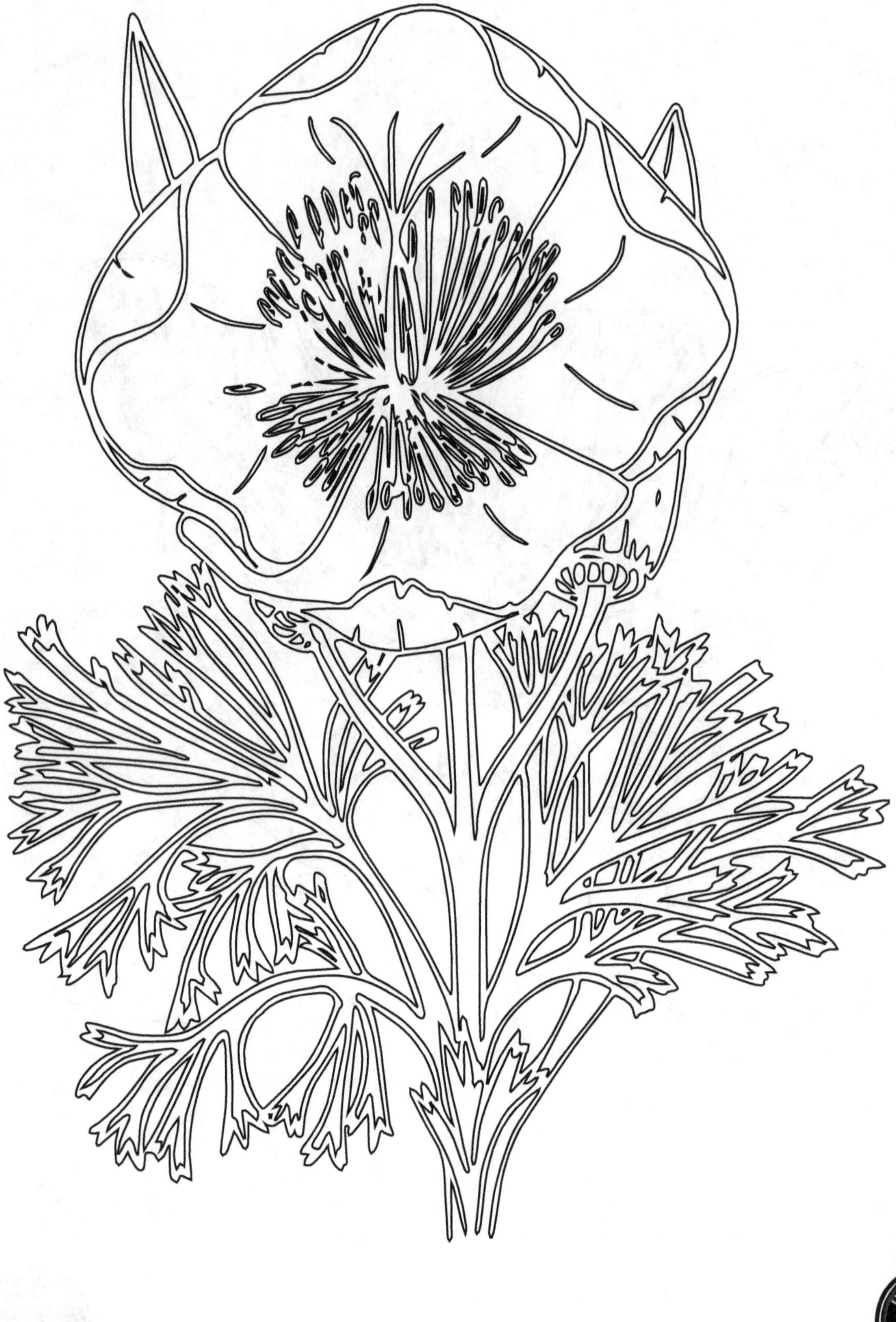

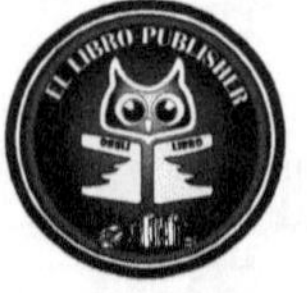

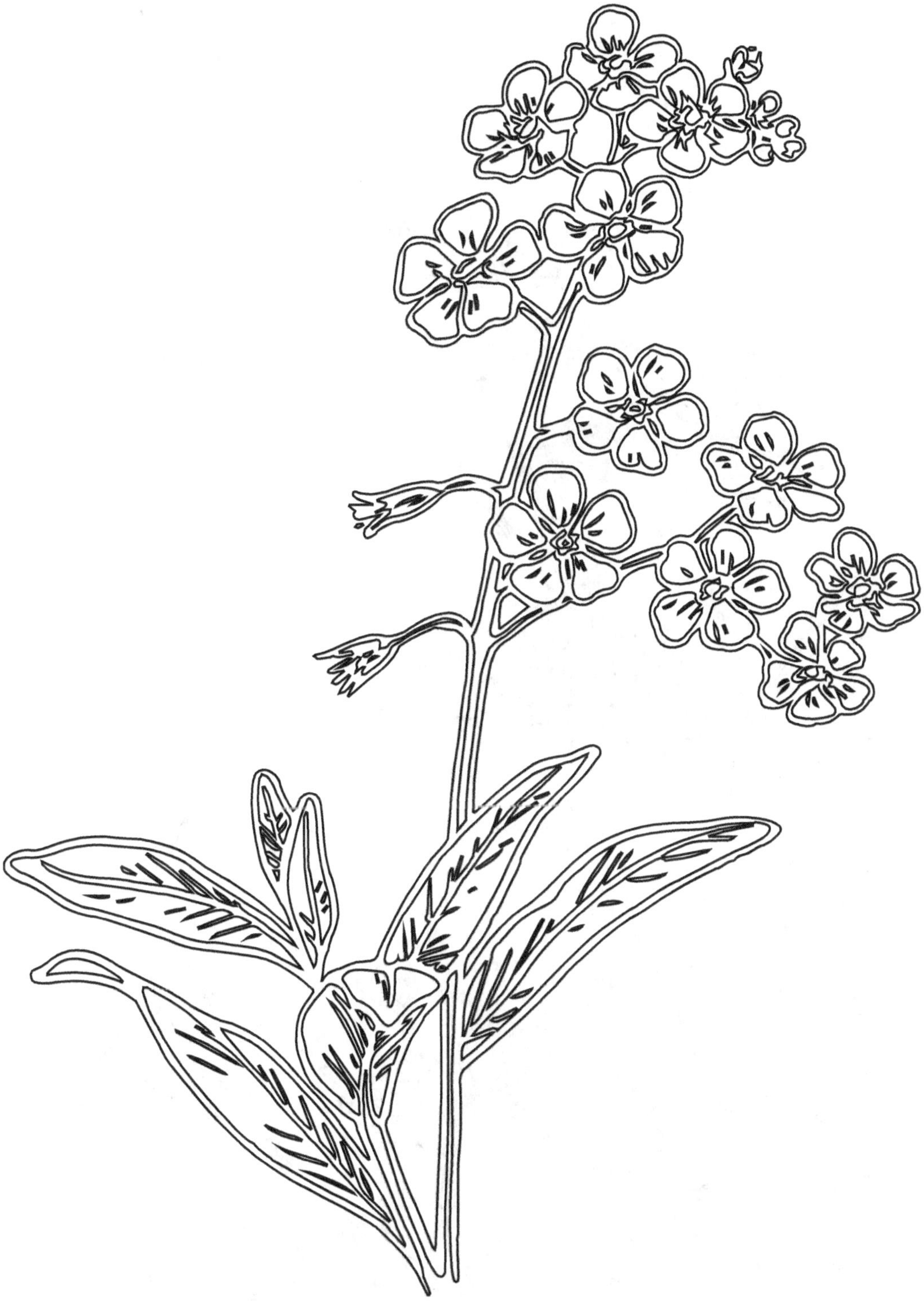

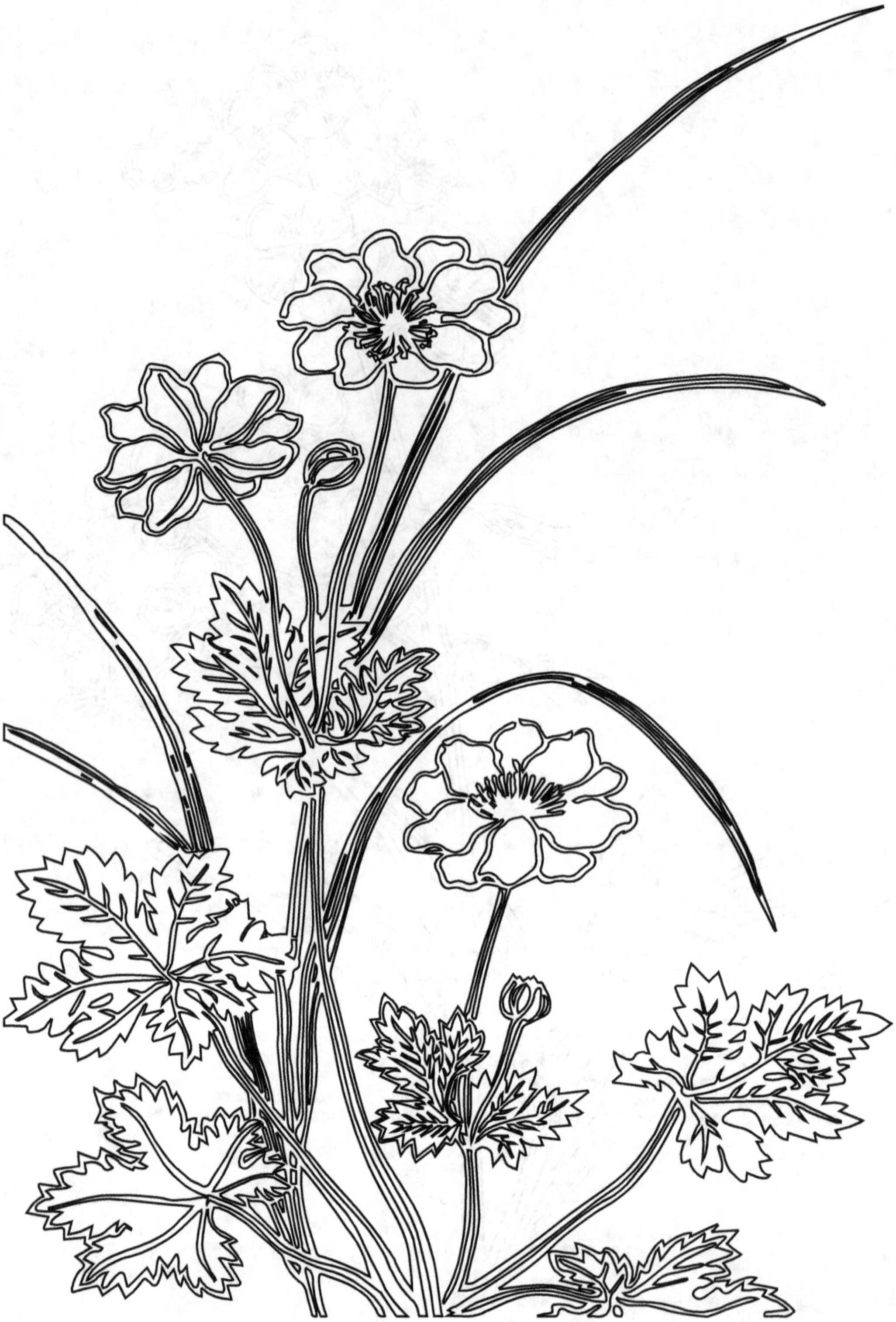

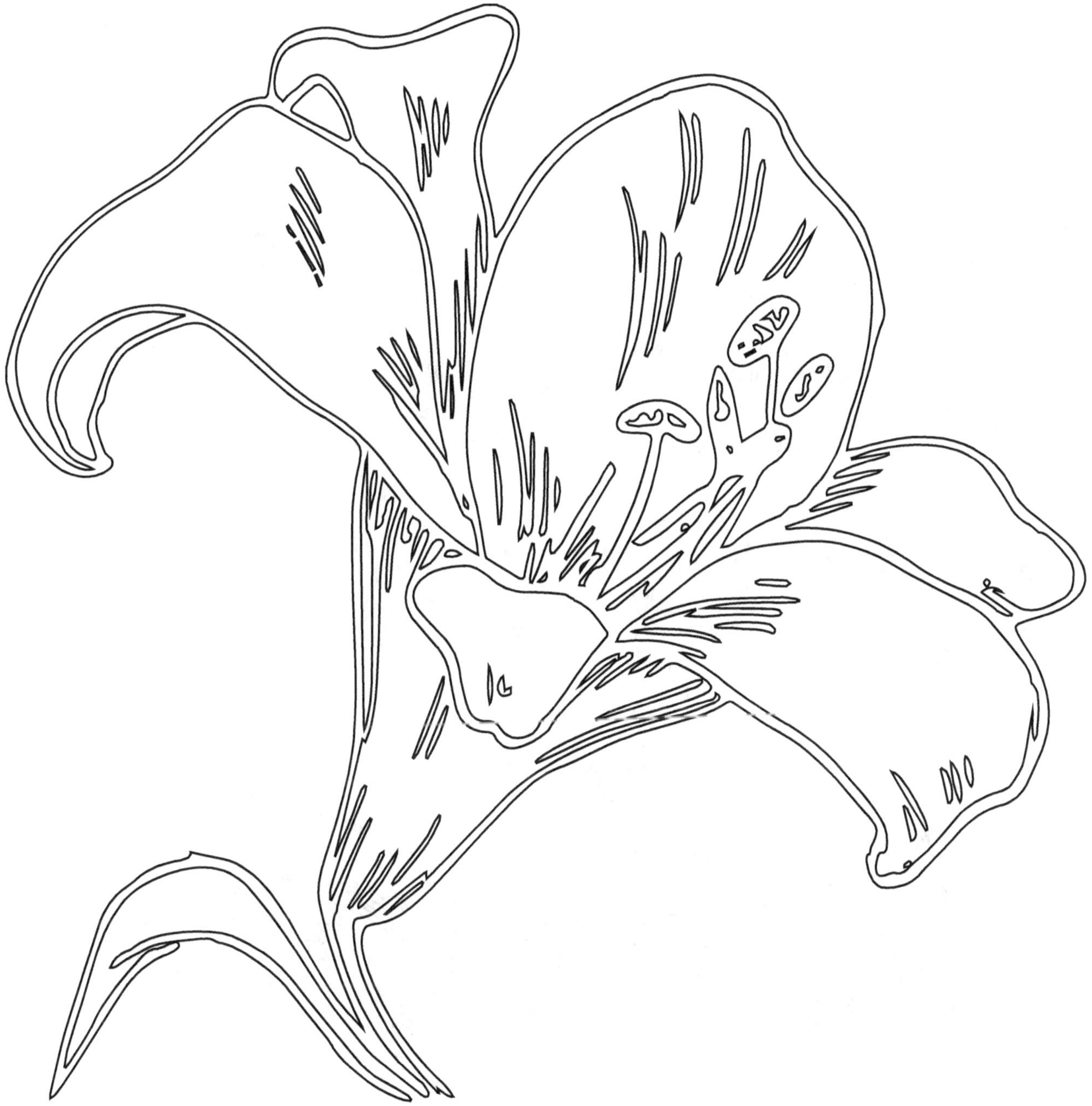

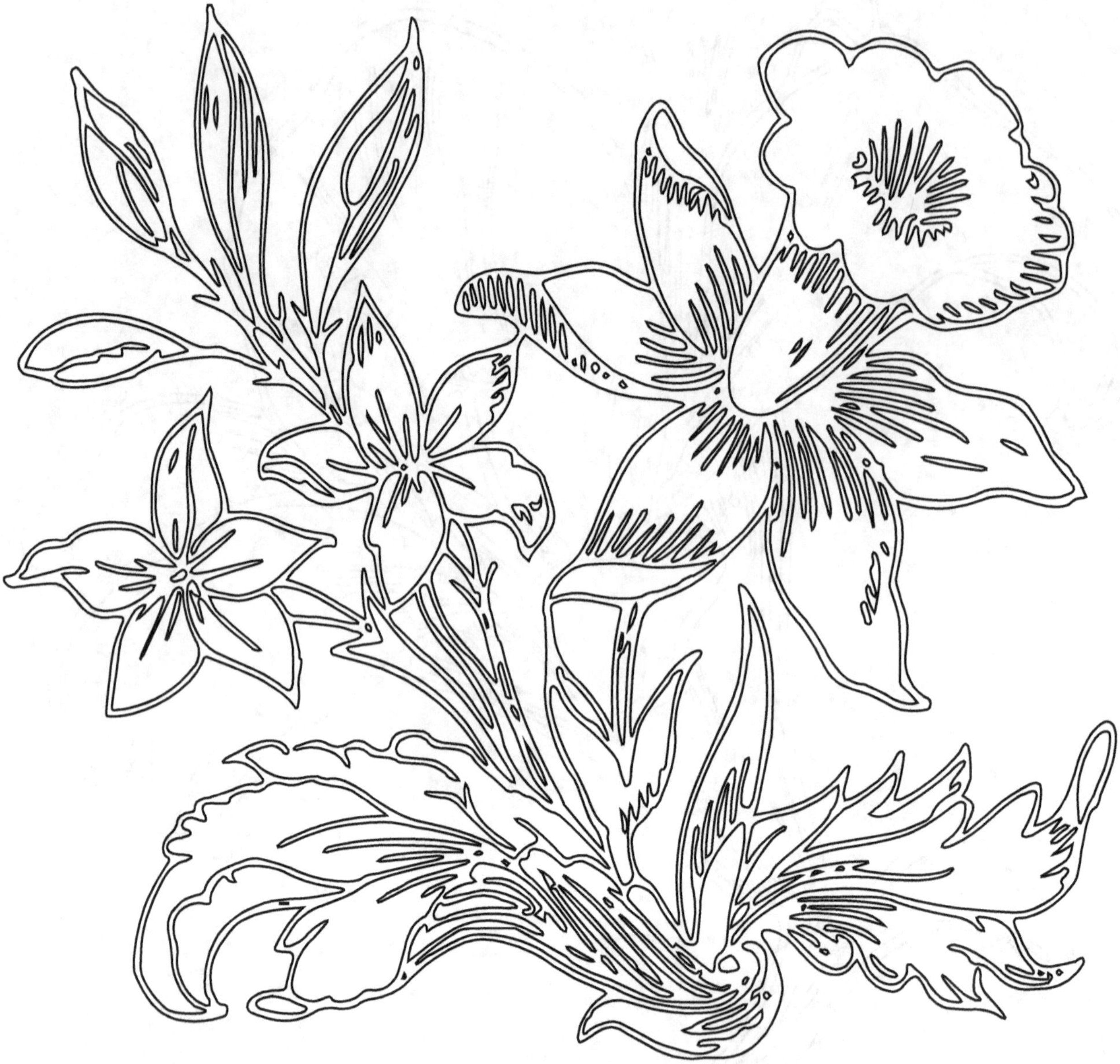

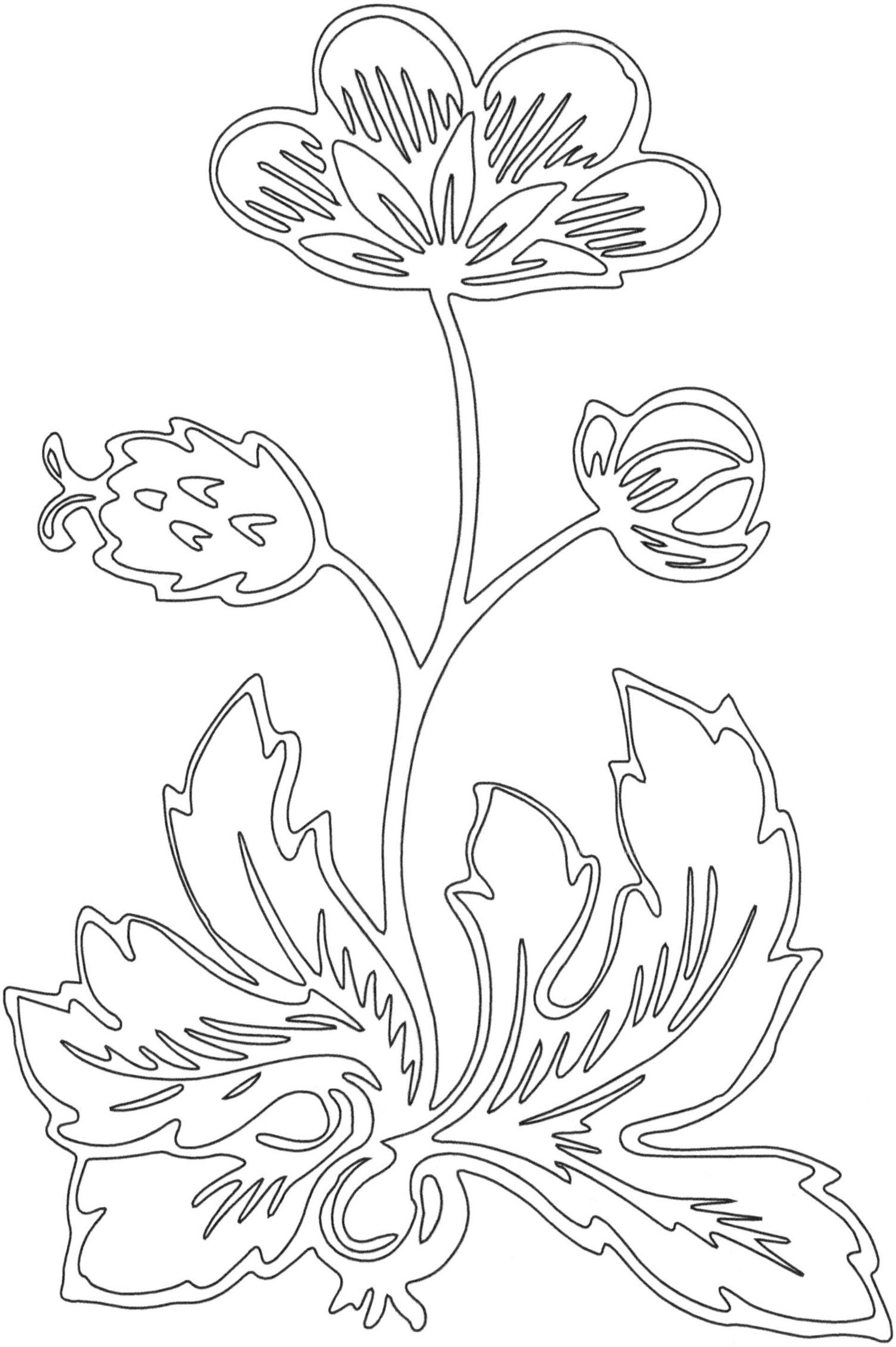

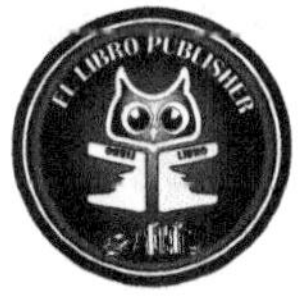

www.ingramcontent.com/pod-product-compliance
Lightning Source LLC
Chambersburg PA
CBHW081544250726

48659CB00009B/3077

9 798418 673138